B Flat, Bebop, Scat

B Flat, Bebop, Scat:
Jazz Short Stories and Poems

Edited by Chris Parker

Drawings by Willa Woolston

Quartet Books
London Melbourne New York

First published by Quartet Books Limited 1986
A member of the Namara Group
27/29 Goodge Street, London W1P 1FD
Copyright © 1986 individual contributors;
illustrations copyright Willa Woolston

British Library Cataloguing in Publication Data
  B flat, bebop, scat: Jazz short stories and poems.
  1. English literature—20th century
  2. Jazz—Literary collections
  I. Parker, Chris
  820.8'0357   PR1111.J/

ISBN 0-7043-2568-3

Typeset by MC Typeset, Chatham, Kent
Printed and bound in Great Britain by
Nene Litho and Woolnough Bookbinding
both of Wellingborough, Northants

Contents

For Red and Mary Lou Callender

The Resurrection of Bobo Jones

William J. Moody

Author-drummer Bill Moody has toured and recorded with Jon Hendricks, Lou Rawls, Maynard Ferguson and Earl 'Fatha' Hines. During 1967–8, he was the only American member of the Gustav Brom Band of Czechoslovakia that toured the Soviet Union, an experience that provided the background for his novel, The Spy Who Played Jazz. He now lives in Las Vegas and teaches at the University of Nevada.

When Brew finally caught up with him, Manny Klein was inhaling spaghetti in a back booth at Chubby's, adding to his already ample girth with pasta and plying a green-eyed blonde called Mary Ann Best with tales of his exploits as New York's premier talent scout. As usual, Manny was exaggerating but probably not about Rocky King.

'The point is,' Manny said, mopping up sauce with a hunk of french bread, 'this time you've gone too far.' He popped the bread in his mouth, wiped his three chins with a white napkin tucked in his collar and gazed at Brew Daniels with the incredulous stare of a small child suddenly confronted with a modern sculpture. 'You're dead, sport. Rocky's put the word out on you. He thinks you're crazy and you know what? So do I.'

Mary Ann watched as Brew grinned sheepishly and shrugged. Nobody had ever called him crazy. A flake definitely, but with jazz musicians, that comes with the territory, where eccentric behaviour is a byword, the foundation of legends.

Everyone knew about Thelonious Monk keeping his piano in the kitchen and Dizzy Gillespie running for president. And who hadn't

1

heard about Sonny Rollins, startling passers-by with the mournful wail of his saxophone when he found the Williamsburg Bridge an inspiring place to practise after he dropped out of the jazz wars for a couple of years.

Strange perhaps, but these, Brew reasoned, were essentially harmless examples that if anything enhanced reputations and merely added another layer to the jazz mystique. With Brew however, it was another story.

Begun modestly, Brew's escapades gradually gathered momentum and eventually exceeded even the hazy boundaries of acceptable behaviour in the jazz world until they threatened to eclipse his considerable skill with a tenor saxophone. Brew had the talent. Nobody denied that. 'One of jazz's most promising newcomers,' wrote one reviewer after witnessing Brew come out on top in a duel with one of the grizzled veterans of the music.

It was Brew's off-stage antics – usually at the expense of his current employer – that got him into trouble, earned him less than the customary two weeks' notice, and branded him a *bona fide* flake. But however outlandish the prank, Brew always felt fully justified even if his victims just as violently disagreed. Brew was selective but no one, not even Brew himself, knew when or where he would be inspired to strike next. Vocalist Dana McKay, for example, never saw Brew coming until it was too late.

Dana McKay is one of those paradoxes all too common in the music business: a very big star with very little talent, although her legions of fans don't seem to notice. Thanks to the marvels of modern recording technology, top-flight studio orchestras and syrupy vocal backgrounds, Miss McKay sounds passable on recordings. Live is another story. She knows it and the bands who back her know it, so when the musicians who hang out at Chubby's heard Brew had consented to sub for an ailing friend at the Americana, the smart money said Brew wouldn't last a week and Dana McKay might be his latest victim. They were right on both counts.

To Brew, the music was bad enough but what really got to him was the phoney sentimentality of her act: shaking hands with the ringsiders, telling the audience how much they meant to her – exactly the same way, every show, every night. Dana McKay could produce tears on cue. Naturally, Brew was inspired.

The third night, he arrived early, armed with a stack of McDonalds' hats and unveiled his brainstorm to the band. They didn't need much persuading. Miss McKay had, as usual, done nothing to endear herself to the musicians. She called unnecessary rehearsals, complained to the conductor, and treated everyone as her personal slave. Except for the lady harpist, even the string section went along.

Timing was essential, so on Brew's cue, at precisely the moment Miss McKay was tugging heartstrings with a teary-eyed rendition of one of her hits, the entire band donned the McDonalds' hats, stood up with arms spread majestically and sang out, 'You deserve a break today!'

When the thunderous chorus struck, Miss McKay never knew what hit her. One of the straps of her gown snapped and almost exposed more of her than planned. She nearly fell off the stage. The dinner-show audience howled with delight, thinking it was part of the show. It got a mention in one of the columns but Miss McKay was not amused.

It took several minutes for the laughter to die down and by that time she'd regained her composure. She smiled mechanically and turned to the band. 'How about these guys, folks? Aren't they something?' Her eyes locked on Brew grinning innocently in the middle of the sax section. She fixed him with an icy glare and Brew was fired before the midnight show. He was never sure how she knew he was responsible but he guessed the lady harpist had a hand in it.

Brew kept a low profile for a while after that, basking in the glory of his most ambitious project to date, and made ends meet with a string of club dates in the Village. It wasn't until he went on the road with Rocky King that he struck again. Everyone agreed Brew was justified this time but for once, he picked on the wrong man.

Rocky King is arguably the most hated bandleader in America, despite his nationwide popularity. Musicians refer to him as a 'legend in his own mind'. He pays only minimum scale, delights in belittling his musicians on the stand, and has been known on occasion physically to assault anyone who doesn't measure up to his often unrealistic expectations. A man to be reckoned with, so when the news got out, Rocky swore a vendetta against Brew that even Manny Klein couldn't diffuse – and he'd got Brew the job.

'C'mon, Manny,' Brew said. 'Rocky had it coming.'

Manny shook his head. 'You hear that, Mary Ann? I get him the best job he's ever had, lay my own reputation on the line and all he can say is Rocky had it coming. Less than a week with the band, he starts a mutiny and puts Rocky King off his own bus forty miles from Indianapolis. You know what your problem is, Brew? Priorities. Your priorities are all wrong.'

Brew stifled a yawn and smiled again at Mary Ann. 'Priorities?'

'Exactly. Now take Mary Ann here. *Her* priorities are in exactly the right place.'

Brew grinned. 'They certainly are.' Mary Ann blushed slightly but Brew caught a flicker of interest in her green eyes. So did Manny.

'I'm warning you, Mary Ann,' Manny said. 'This is a dangerous man, bent on self-destruction. Don't be misled by that angelic face.' Manny took out an evil-looking cigar, lit it and puffed on it furiously until the booth was enveloped in a cloud of smoke.

'Did you really do that? Put Rocky off the bus?' Mary Ann asked.

Brew shrugged and flicked a glance at Manny. 'Not exactly the way Manny tells it. As usual, he's left out a few minor details.' Brew leaned in closer to her. 'One of the trumpet players had quit, see. His wife was having a baby and he wanted to get home in time. But kind, generous Rocky King wouldn't let him ride on the bus even though we had to pass right through his home town. So, when we stopped for gas, I managed to lock Rocky in the men's room and told the driver he'd be joining us later. It seemed like the right thing to do at the time.'

'And what has it got you?' Manny said, emerging from the smoke, annoyed to see Mary Ann was laughing. 'Nothing but your first and last cheque, minus of course Rocky's taxi fare to Indianapolis. You're an untouchable now. You'll be lucky to get a wedding at Roseland.'

Brew shuddered. Roseland was the massive ballroom under the Musicians' Union and the site of a Wednesday-afternoon ritual known as cattle call. Hundreds of musicians jam the ballroom as casual contractors call for one instrument at a time. 'I need a piano player for Saturday night.' Fifty pianists or drummers or whatever is called rush the stage. First one there gets the gig.

'Did the trumpet player get home in time?' Mary Ann asked.

'What? Oh yeah. It was a boy.'

'Well I think it was a nice thing to do.' She looked challengingly at Manny.

'OK, OK,' Manny said, accepting defeat. 'So you're the good samaritan but you're still out of work and I . . .' He paused for a moment, his face creasing into a baleful smile. 'There is one thing . . . naw, you wouldn't be interested.'

'C'mon, Manny, I'm interested. Anything's better than Roseland.'

Manny shrugged. 'Well, I don't know if it's still going, but I heard they were looking for a tenor player at the Final Bar.'

Brew groaned and slumped back against the seat. 'The Final Bar is a toilet. A lot of people don't even know it's still there.'

'Exactly,' said Manny. 'The ideal place for you at the moment.' He blew out another cloud of smoke and studied the end of his cigar. 'Bobo Jones is there, with a trio.'

'Bobo Jones? *The* Bobo Jones?'

'The same, but don't get excited. We both know Bobo hasn't played a note worth listening to in years. A guy named Rollo runs the place. I'll give him a call if you think you can cut it. Sorry sport,

4

that's the best I can do.'

'Yeah, do that,' Brew said dazedly, but something in Manny's smile told Brew he'd be sorry. He was vaguely aware of Mary Ann asking for directions as he made his way out of Chubby's. So it had come to this. The Final Bar.

He couldn't imagine Bobo Jones there.

The winos had begun to sing.

Brew watched them from across the aisle. Two lost souls, arms draped over each other, wine dribbling down their chins as they happily crooned off-key between belts from a bottle in a paper bag. Except for an immense black woman, Brew and the winos were alone as the Seventh Avenue subway hurtled towards the Village.

'This city ain't fit to live in no more,' the woman shouted over the roar of the train. She had a shopping-bag wedged between her knees and scowled at the winos.

Brew nodded in agreement and glanced at the ceiling where someone had spray-painted, 'Puerto Rico – Independencia!' in jagged red letters. Priorities Manny had said. For once maybe he was right. Introspection was not one of Brew's qualities but maybe it was time. Even one-nighters with Rocky King was better than the Final Bar.

The winos finally passed out after 42nd Street but a wiry Latin kid in a leather jacket swaggered on to the car and instantly eyed Brew's horn. Brew figured him for a terrorist or at least a mugger. It was going to be his horn or the black woman's shopping-bag.

Brew picked up his horn and hugged it protectively to his chest, then gave the kid his best glare. Even with his height, there was little about Brew to inspire fear. Shaggy blond curls over a choirboy face and deep-set blue eyes didn't worry the Puerto Rican kid, who Brew figured probably had an eleven-inch blade under his jacket.

They had a staring contest until 14th Street when Brew's plan became clear. He waited until the last possible second, then shot off the train like a firing-squad was at his back. He paused just long enough on the platform to smile at the kid staring at him through the doors as the train pulled away.

'Faggot!' the kid yelled. Brew turned and sprinted up the steps wondering why people thought it was so much fun to live in New York.

Outside, he turned up his collar against the frosty air and plunged into the mass of humanity that makes New York look like an evacuation. He elbowed his way across the street, splashing through grey piles of slush that clung to the curbs, soaked shoes and provided cabbies with opportunities to practise their favourite winter pastime of splattering pedestrians. He turned off Seventh Avenue, long legs eating up the pavement, and tried again to envision Bobo Jones at the Final Bar, but it was impossible.

For as long as Brew could remember, Bobo Jones had been one of the legendary figures of jazz piano, one of the giants. Bud Powell, Monk, Oscar Peterson – hell, Bobo *was* a jazz piano. But Bobo's career, if brilliant, had also been stormy, laced with bizarre incidents, culminating one night at the Village Vanguard during a live recording session. Before a horrified opening-night audience, Bobo had attacked and nearly killed his saxophone player.

Midway through the first tune, the crazed Bobo had leapt wild-eyed from the piano, screamed something unintelligible and pounced on the unsuspecting saxophonist, who thought he had at least two more choruses to play. Bobo wrestled him to the floor and all but strangled him with the microphone cord. The saxophonist was already gagging on his mouthpiece and in the end suffered enough throat-damage to cause him to switch to guitar. He eventually quit music altogether and went into business with his brother-in-law selling insurance in New Jersey.

Juice Wilson, Bobo's two-hundred-and-forty-pound drummer, had never moved so fast in his life unless it was the time he'd mistakenly wandered into a Ku Klux Klan meeting in his native Alabama. Juice dived over the drums, sending one of his cymbals flying into a ringside table full of Rotarians. He managed to pull Bobo off the gasping saxophonist with the help of two cops who hated jazz anyway. A waiter called the paramedics and the saxophonist was given emergency treatment under the piano while the audience looked on in stunned disbelief.

One member of the audience was a photographer for *Time* magazine, showing his out-of-town girlfriend the sights of New York. He knew a scoop when he saw it, whipped out his camera, and snapped off a dozen quick ones while Juice and the cops tried to subdue Bobo. The following week's issue ran a photo of Bobo, glassy-eyed in a straitjacket with the caption: 'Is This the End of Jazz?' The two cops hoped so because they were in the photo too and their watch commander wanted to know what the hell they were doing in a jazz club if they hadn't busted any dopers.

The critics in the audience shook their empty heads and claimed they'd seen it coming for a long time as Bobo was taken away to Bellevue. Fans and friends alike mourned the passing of a great talent but everyone was sure Bobo would recover. He never did.

Bobo spent three months in Bellevue, playing silent chords on the wall of his padded cell and confounding the doctors who could find nothing wrong with him, so naturally, they diagnosed him as manic-depressive and put him back on the street. With all the other loonies in New York, one more wouldn't make any difference.

Bobo disappeared for nearly a year after that. No one knew or cared how he survived. Most people assumed he was living on the royalties from the dozen or so albums he'd left as a legacy to his many fans. But then, he mysteriously reappeared. There were rumours of a comeback. Devoted fans sought him out in obscure clubs, patiently waiting for the old magic to return. But it seemed gone for ever. Gradually, all but the most devout drifted away, until, if the cardboard sign in the window could be believed, Bobo Jones was apparently condemned at last to the Final Bar.

Brew knew that much of the story but if he'd known the why of Bobo's downfall, he would have gone straight back to the subway, looked up the Puerto Rican kid and given him his horn. That would have been easier. Instead, he sidestepped a garbage can and pushed through the door of the Final Bar.

A gust of warm air, reeking of stale smoke and warm beer, washed over him. Dark, dirty and foul-smelling, the Final Bar is every Hollywood scriptwriter's idea of a Greenwich Village jazz club. To musicians, it means a tiny, poorly lit bandstand, an ancient upright piano with broken keys and never more than seven customers if you count the bartender.

Musicians play at the Final Bar in desperation, on the way up. For Bobo Jones, and now perhaps Brew Daniels as well, the Final Bar is the last stop on the downward spiral to oblivion. But there he was, one of the legends of jazz. One glance told Brew all he needed to know. Bobo was down, way down.

He sat slumped at the piano, head bent, nearly touching the keyboard and played like a man trying to recall how he used to sound. Lost in the past, his head would occasionally jerk up in response to some dimly remembered phrase that just as quickly snuffed out. His fingers flew over the keys frantically in pursuit of lost magic. A forgotten cigarette burned on top of the piano next to an empty glass.

To Bobo's right were bassist Deacon Hayes and drummer Juice Wilson, implacable sentinels guarding some now-forgotten treasure. They brought to mind a black Laurel and Hardy. Deacon, rail-thin and solemn-faced, occasionally arched an eyebrow. Juice, dwarfing his drums, stared ahead blankly and languidly stroked the cymbals. They had remained loyal to the end and this was apparently it.

Brew was mesmerized by the scene. He watched and listened and slowly shook his head in disbelief. A knife of fear crept into his gut. He recognized with sudden awareness the clear, unmistakable qualities that hovered around the bandstand like a thick fog: despair and failure.

Brew wanted to run. He'd seen enough. Manny's message was clear but now, a wave of anger swept over him, forcing him to stay. He spun around towards the bar and saw what could only be Rollo draped over a bar stool. A skinny black man in a beret, chin in hand, staring vacantly at the hapless trio.

'You Rollo? I'm Brew Daniels.' Rollo's only response was to cross his legs. 'Manny call you?'

Rollo moved only his eyes, inspected Brew, found him wanting and shifted his gaze back to the bandstand. 'You the tenor player?' he asked contemptuously.

'Who were you expecting, Stan Getz?' Brew shot back. He wanted to leave, just forget the whole thing. He didn't belong here but he had to prove it. To Manny and himself.

'You ain't funny, man,' Rollo said. 'Check with Juice.'

Brew nodded and turned back to the bandstand. The music had stopped but Brew had no idea what they had played. They probably didn't either, he thought. What difference did it make? He tugged at Juice's arm dangling near the floor.

'OK if I play a couple?' Brew asked.

Juice squinted at Brew suspiciously, took in his horn case and gave a shrug that Brew took as reluctant permission. He unzipped the leather bag and took out a gleaming tenor saxophone.

He knew why Manny had sent him down here. There was no gig. This was just a lesson in humility. It would be like blowing in a graveyard.

He put the horn together, decided against even asking anyone to tune up and blew a couple of tentative phrases. ' "Green Dolphin Street", OK?'

Bobo looked up from the piano and stared at Brew like he was a bug on a windshield. 'Whozat?' he asked, pointing a long, slim finger. His voice was a gravelly whisper, like Louis Armstrong with a cold.

'I *think* he's a tenor player,' Juice said defiantly. 'He's gonna play *one*.' Bobo had already lost interest.

Brew glared at Juice. He was mad now and in a hurry. Deacon's eyebrows arched as Brew snapped his fingers for the tempo. Then he was off, on the run from despair.

Knees bent, chest heaving, body rocking slightly, Brew tore into the melody and ripped it apart. The horn, jutting out of his mouth like another limb, spewed fire. Harsh abrasive tones of anger and frustration that washed over the unsuspecting patrons – there were five tonight – like napalm, grabbing them by the throat and saying,

'Listen to this, dammit!'

At the bar, Rollo gulped and nearly fell off the stool. In spite of occasional lapses in judgement, Rollo liked to think of himself as a jazz critic. He'd never fully recovered from his Ornette Coleman blunder. For seventeen straight nights, he'd sat sphinx-like at the Five Spot watching the black man with the white plastic saxophone before finally declaring, 'Nothin', baby. Ornette ain't playin' nothin'.' But this time there was no mistake. In a bursting flash of recognition, Rollo knew.

Brew had taken everyone by surprise. Deacon's eyebrows were shooting up and down like windshield wipers. Juice crouched behind his drums and slashed at the cymbals like a fencer. They heard it too. They knew.

Brew played like a backup quarterback in the final two minutes of the last game of the year with his team behind seventeen to nothing. He ripped off jagged chunks of sound and slung them about the Final Bar leaving Juice and Deacon to scurry after him in desperate pursuit. During his last scorching chorus, he pointed the bell of his horn at Bobo, prodding, challenging, until he at last backed away.

Bobo reacted like a man under siege. He'd begun as always, staring at the keyboard as if it were a giant puzzle he'd forgotten how to solve. But by Brew's third chorus, he seized the lifeline offered and struggled to pull himself out of the past. Eyes closed, head thrown back, his fingers flew over the keys, producing a barrage of notes that nearly matched Brew's.

Deacon and Juice exchanged glances. Where had they heard this before? Rollo, off the stool, rocked and grinned in pure joy.

'Shee–it!' he yelled.

Bobo was back.

By the end of the first week, word had got around. Something was happening at the Final Bar and people were dropping in to see if the rumours were true. Bobo Jones had climbed out of his shell and was not only playing again but presenting a reasonable facsimile of his former talent, inspired apparently by a fiery young tenor saxophonist. It didn't matter that Brew had been on the scene for some time. He was ironically being heralded as a new discovery. But even that didn't bother Brew. He was relaxed.

The music and his life were, at least for the moment, under control. Mary Ann was a regular at the club – she hadn't signed with Manny after all – and by the end of the month, they were sharing her tiny Westside apartment.

But gnawing around the edges were the strange looks Brew caught

from Deacon and Juice. They'd look away quickly and mumble to themselves while Rollo showed Brew only the utmost respect. Bobo was the enigma, either remaining totally aloof or smothering Brew with attentive concern, following him around the club like a shadow. If Brew found it stifling or even creepy, he wisely wrote it off as the pianist's awkward attempt at gratitude and reminded himself that Bobo had spent three months in a mental ward.

Of his playing, however, there was no doubt. For some unknown reason, Brew's horn had unlocked Bobo's past, unleashing the old magic that flew off Bobo's fingers with nightly improvement. Brew himself was as big a benefactor to Bobo's resurgence as his own playing reached new heights. His potential was at last being realized. He was loose, making it with a good gig, a good woman and life had never been sweeter. Naturally, that's when the trouble began.

They were curled up watching the late movie when Brew heard the buzzer. Opening the door, Brew found Bobo standing in the hall, half hidden in a topcoat several sizes too large, a stack of records under his arm.

'Got something for you to hear, man,' Bobo rasped, walking past Brew to look for the stereo.

'Hey, Bobo, you know what time it is?'

'Yeah, it's twenty after four.' Bobo was crouched in front of the stereo, looking through the records.

Brew nodded and shut the door. 'That's what I thought you'd say.' He went into the bedroom. Mary Ann was sitting up in bed.

'Who is it?'

'Bobo,' Brew said, grabbing a robe. 'He's got some records he wants me to hear. I gotta humour him I guess.'

'Does he know what time it is?'

'Yeah, twenty after four.'

Mary Ann looked at him quizzically. 'I'll make some coffee,' she said, slipping out of bed.

Brew sighed and went back to the living-room. Bobo had one of the records on the turntable and was kneeling with his head up against the speaker. The record was one of his early ones with a tenor player called Lee Evans, a name only vaguely familiar to Brew.

Brew had studiously avoided the trap of listening to other tenor players except maybe for John Coltrane. No tenor player could avoid that, but his style was forged largely on his own. A mixture of hard brittle fluidness on up tempos, balanced by an effortless shifting of gears for lyrical ballads – a cross between Sonny Rollins and Stan Getz. But there was something familiar about this record, something he couldn't quite place.

'I want to do this tune tonight,' Bobo said, turning his eyes to

11

Brew. It was the first time Bobo had made any direct reference to the music.

Brew nodded absently, absorbed in the music. What was it? He focused on the tenor player and only vaguely remembered Mary Ann coming in with the coffee. Much later the record was still playing and Mary Ann was curled up in a ball on the couch. Early-morning sun streamed in the window. Bobo was gone.

'You know, it's funny,' Brew told her later. 'I kinda sound like that tenor player, Lee Evans.'

'What happened to him?'

'I don't know. He played with Bobo quite a while but I think he was killed in a car accident. I'll ask Rollo. Maybe he knows.'

But if Rollo knew, he wasn't saying. Neither were Juice or Deacon. He avoided asking Bobo, sensing it was somehow a taboo subject, but it was clear they all knew something he didn't. It became an obsession for Brew.

He nearly wore out the records Bobo had left and unconsciously, more and more of Lee Evans's style crept into his own playing. It seemed to please Bobo and brought approving nods from Juice and Deacon. As far as Brew could remember, he'd never heard Lee Evans until the night Bobo had brought the records but damned if he didn't sound very much the same. Finally, he could stand it no longer and pressed Rollo. He had to know.

'Man, why you wanna mess things up for now?' Rollo asked, avoiding Brew's eyes. 'Bobo's playin', the club's busy and you gettin' famous.'

'C'mon, Rollo, I only asked about Lee Evans. What's the big secret?' Brew was puzzled by the normally docile Rollo's outburst and intrigued even more. However tenuous Bobo's return to reality, Brew couldn't see the connection. Not yet.

'Aw shit,' Rollo said, slamming down a bar rag. 'You best see Razor.'

'Who the hell's Razor?'

'Wunna the players, man. Got hisself some ladies and he's . . . well, you talk to him if you want.'

'I want,' Brew said, more puzzled than ever.

But Mary Ann was not so sure. 'You may not like what you find,' she warned. Her words were like a prophecy.

Brew found Razor off 10th Avenue.

A massive maroon Buick idled at the curb. Nearby, Razor, in an ankle-length fur coat and matching hat, peered at one of his 'ladies' from behind dark glasses. But what really got Brew's attention was the dog. Sitting majestically at Razor's heel, sinewy neck encased in a silver stud collar was the biggest, most vicious-looking Doberman Brew had ever seen. About then, Brew wanted to forget the whole thing but he was frozen to the spot as Razor's dog – he hoped it was Razor's dog – bared his teeth, growled throatily and locked his dark eyes on Brew.

Razor's lady, in white plastic boots, mini-skirt and a ski jacket, cowered against a building. Tears streamed down her face, smearing garish make-up. Her eyes were locked on the black man as he fondled a pearl-handled straight razor. Brew had never seen anyone so frightened.

'Lookee here, mama, you makin' old Razor mad with all this talk about you leavin', and you know what happen when Razor get mad right?' The girl nodded slowly as he opened and closed the razor several times before finally dropping it in his pocket. 'Aw right then,' Razor said. 'Git on outta here.' The girl glanced briefly at Brew then scurried away.

'Whatchu lookin' at, honky?' Razor asked, turning his attention to Brew. Several people passed by them, looking straight ahead as if they didn't exist.

Brew's throat was dry. He could hardly get the words out. 'Uh, I'm Brew Daniels . . . I play with Bobo at the Final Bar. Rollo said – '

'Bobo? Shee–it.' Razor slapped his leg and laughed, throwing his head back. 'Yeah, I hear that sucker's playin' again.' He took off the glasses and studied Brew closely. 'And you the cat that jarred them old bones. Man, you don't even look like a musician.'

The Doberman cocked his head and looked at Razor as if that might be a signal to eat Brew. 'Be cool, Honey,' Razor said, stroking the dog's sleek head. 'Well, you must play, man. C'mon, it's gettin' cold talkin' to these bitches out here. I know what you want.' He opened the door of the Buick. 'C'mon, Honey, we goin' for a ride.'

Brew sat rigidly in front, trying to decide who scared him more, Razor or the dog. He could feel Honey's warm breath on the back of his neck. 'Nice dog you got, Mr Razor,' he said. Honey only growled and Razor didn't speak until they pulled up near Riverside Park.

He threw open the door and Honey scrambled out. 'Go on, Honey. Git one of them suckers.' Honey barked and bounded away in pursuit of a pair of unsuspecting Cocker Spaniels.

Razor took out cigarettes from a platinum case, lit two with a gold lighter and passed one to Brew. 'It was about three years ago,' Razor began. 'Bobo was hot and he had this bad-assed tenor called Lee Evans. They was really tight. Lee was just a kid but Bobo took care of him like he was his daddy. Anyway, they was giggin' in Detroit or some place, just before they was spozed to open here. But Lee, man,

13

he had him some action he wanted to check out on the way so he drove on alone. He got loaded at this chick's pad, then tried to drive all night to make the gig.' Razor took a deep drag on his cigarette. 'Went to sleep. His car went right off the pike into a gas station. Boom! That was it.'

Razor fell silent. Brew swallowed as the pieces began to fall into place.

'Well, they didn't tell Bobo what happened till an hour before the gig and them jive-ass, faggot record dudes said seein' as how they'd already given Bobo front money, he had to do the session. They got another dude on tenor. He was bad but he wasn't Lee Evans. At first, Bobo was cool, like he didn't know what was happening. Then all of a sudden, he jumped on this cat — scared his ass good, screamin' "You ain't Lee, you ain't Lee." ' Razor shook his head and flipped his cigarette out the window.

Brew closed his eyes. It was so quiet in the car Brew was sure he could hear his own heart beating, as everything came together. All the pieces fell into place except one but he had to ask: 'What's this all got to do with me?'

Razor turned to him, puzzled. 'Man, you is one dumb honky. Don't you see, man? To Bobo, you is Lee Evans all over again. Must be how you blow.'

'But I'm not,' Brew protested, feeling panic rise in him. 'Someone's got to tell him I'm not.'

Razor's eyes narrowed, his voice lowered menacingly. 'Ain't nobody got to tell nobody nothin'. Bobo was sick for a long time. If he's playin' again cause of you, that's enuff. You,' he pointed a finger at Brew, 'jus' be cool and blow your horn.' There was no mistake. It was an order.

'But . . .'

'But nothin'. And if there's anything else goin' down, I'll hear about it. Who do you think took care of Bobo? You know my name, man? Jones. Razor Jones.' He smiled suddenly at Brew. 'Bobo is my brother.'

Razor started the car and whistled for Honey. Brew got out slowly and stood at the curb like a survivor of the holocaust. The huge Doberman galloped back obediently, sniffed at Brew and jumped in the car next to Razor.

'Bye,' Razor called, flashing Brew a toothy smile. Brew could swear Honey sneered at him as the car drove away.

The Final Bar was now the in place in the Village. Manny had seen to that, forgiving Brew for all his past sins and recognizing Bobo's return, if artfully managed, would insure all their futures. Manny was pragmatic if nothing else. He was on the phone daily, negotiating with record companies and spreading the word that a great event in jazz was about to take place.

Driven by the memory of Razor's menacing smile, Brew played like a man possessed, astonishing musicians who came in to hear for themselves. He was getting calls from people he'd never heard of, offering record dates, road tours, even to form his own group. But of course Brew wasn't going anywhere. He was miserable.

'You sound great, kid,' Manny said, looking around the club. It was packed every night now and Rollo had hired extra help to handle the increase in business. 'Listen, wait till you hear the deal I've made with Newport Records. A live session, right here. The return of Bobo Jones. Of course, I insisted on top billing for you too.' Manny was beaming. 'How about that, eh?'

'I think I'll go to Paris,' Brew said, staring ahead vacantly.

'Paris?' Manny turned to Mary Ann. 'What's he talking about?'

Mary Ann shrugged. 'He's got this crazy idea about Bobo.'

'What's the idea? Brew, talk to me,' Manny said.

'I mean,' Brew said evenly, 'there isn't going to be any record. Not with me anyway.'

Manny's face fell. 'No record? Whatta you mean? An album with Bobo will make you. At the risk of sounding like an agent, this is your big break.'

'Manny, you don't understand. Bobo thinks I'm Lee Evans. Don't you see?'

'No, I don't see,' Manny said, glaring at Brew. 'I don't care if he thinks you're Jesus Christ with a saxophone. We're talking major bucks here. Big. Blow this one and you might as well sell your horn.' Manny turned back pleadingly to Mary Ann. 'For God's sake, Mary Ann, talk some sense to him, will you?'

Mary Ann shrugged. 'He's afraid Bobo will flip out again and he's worried about Bobo's brother.'

'Yeah, Manny, you would be too if you saw him. He's got the biggest razor I've ever seen. And if that isn't enough, he's got a killer dog that would just love to tear me to pieces.'

'What did you do to him? You're not up to your old tricks again?'

'No, no, nothing. He just told me, ordered me, to keep playing with Bobo.'

'So what's the problem?'

Brew sighed. 'Look, Manny, for one thing, I don't like being a ghost. And what if Bobo attacks me like the last time? He almost killed that guy. Bobo needs to be told but no one will do it and I *can't* do it. So it's Bobo, Razor or Paris. I'll take Paris. I've heard there's a good jazz scene there.'

Manny looked dumbly at Mary Ann. 'Is he serious? C'mon, Brew, that's ridiculous. Look, Newport wants to set this up for next Monday night and I'm warning you. Screw this up and I will personally see that you never work again.' He laughed then and slapped Brew on the back. 'It'll be all right, Brew. Trust me.'

But Brew didn't trust anyone and no one could convince him. Even Mary Ann couldn't get through to him. Finally, he decided to get some expert advice. He checked with Bellevue but was told the case couldn't be discussed unless he was a relative. He even tracked down the saxophonist Bobo had attacked but as soon as he mentioned Bobo's name, the guy slammed down the phone on him. In desperation, Brew remembered a guy he'd met at one of the clubs. A jazz buff, Ted Fisher was doing his internship in psychiatry at Colombia Medical School. Musicians called him Doctor Deep. Brew telephoned, explained what he wanted and they agreed to meet at Chubby's.

'What is this, a gay bar?' Ted Fisher asked, looking around the crowded bar.

'No, Ted, there just aren't a lot of lady musicians. Now look, I – '

'Hey, isn't that Gerry Mulligan over there at the bar?'

'Ted, c'mon. This is serious.'

'Sorry, Brew. Well, from what you've told me already, as I understand it, your concern is that Bobo thinks you're his former saxophone player, right?'

Brew looked desperate. 'I don't think it, I *know* it. Look, Bobo attacked the substitute horn player. What I want to know is what happens if the same conditions are repeated? Bobo's convinced I'm Lee Evans now, but what if the live recording session brings it all back and he suddenly realizes I'm not? Could he flip again and go for me?' Brew sat back and rubbed his throat.

'Hmmm . . .' Ted murmured, staring at the ceiling. 'No, I wouldn't think so. Bobo's fixation, brought about by the loss of a close friend, whom he'd actually, though inadvertently, assumed a father-figure role for is understandable and quite plausible. As for a repeated occurrence, even in simulated, identical conditions, well, delayed shock would account for the first instance, but no. I don't think it's within the realms of possibility.' Ted smiled at Brew reassuringly and lit his pipe.

'Could you put that in a little plainer terms?'

'No, I don't think it would happen again.'

'You're sure?' Brew was already feeling better.

'Yes, absolutely. Unless . . .'

Brew's head snapped up. 'Unless what?'

'Well, unless this Bobo fellow suddenly decided he . . . he didn't like the way you played. Brew? You OK? You look a little pale.'

Brew leaned forward on the table and covered his face with his hands. 'Thanks, Ted,' he whispered.

Ted smiled. 'Any time, Brew. Don't mention it. Hey, do you think Gerry Mulligan would mind if I asked him for his autograph?'

In the end, Brew finally agreed to do the session. It wasn't Manny's insistence or threats. They paled in comparison with Razor. It wasn't even Mary Ann's reasoning. She was convinced Bobo was totally sane. No, in the end, it was the dreams that did it. Always the dreams.

A giant Doberman, wearing sunglasses and carrying a straight razor in its mouth was chasing him through Central Park. In the distance Razor stood holding his horn, laughing. Brew had little choice.

On one point, however, Brew stood firm. The Newport Record executives had taken one look at the Final Bar and almost cancelled the entire deal. They wanted to move the session to the Village Vanguard but Brew figured that was tempting fate too much. Through Mary Ann, Bobo had deferred the final decision to Brew and as far as he was concerned, it was the Final Bar or nothing. The Newport people finally conceded and set about refurbishing the broken-down club. Brew had to admit someone had really spent some money.

The club was completely transformed. It was repainted, new tables were added, blow-up photos of jazz greats were plastered on the walls and the sawdust floor was replaced with new carpeting.

When Brew and Mary Ann arrived, they were greeted at the door by Rollo, nattily attired in a tuxedo, collecting a hefty admission charge, and looking as smart as any maître d' in New York. 'My man Brew,' he smiled, slapping Brew's palm. 'Tonight's the night!'

'Yeah, tonight's the night,' Brew mumbled as they pushed through the crowd. The club was jammed with fans, reporters and photographers. Manny waved to them from the bar where he was huddled with the Newport people. A Steinway grand had replaced the ancient upright piano and a tuner was making final adjustments as engineers scurried about running cables and testing microphones.

Brew suddenly felt a tug at his sleeve. He turned to see Razor, resplendent in a yellow velvet suit, sitting with a matching pair of leggy blondes. Honey hovered nearby. Razor flashed a smile at Mary

Ann and nodded to Brew. 'I see you been keepin' cool. This your lady?'

Brew stepped around Honey, wondering if it were true that dogs can smell fear. 'Yeah. Mary Ann, this is Razor.'

Razor bowed deeply and kissed Mary Ann's hand, then stepped back to introduce the blondes. 'Say hello to Sandra and Shana.'

'Hi,' the blondes chorused in unison.

'What are you doing here?' Brew asked Razor.

'What am *I* doin' here. Man, this is my club. Didn't you know that?' He flashed Brew another smile. 'You play good now.'

In a daze, Brew found Mary Ann a seat near the bandstand. As the piano-tuner finished, a tall man in glasses and a three-piece suit walked to the microphone and introduced himself as the Vice President of Newport Records. He called for quiet, perhaps the first time it had ever been necessary at the Final Bar.

'Ladies and gentlemen, as you all know, we are recording live here tonight so we'd appreciate your co-operation. Right now though, let's give a great big welcome to truly, one of the giants of jazz, Mr Bobo Jones and his quartet.'

The applause was warm and real as they took the stand. Bobo, Deacon and Juice were immaculate in matching tuxes. Brew was dressed likewise but at the last minute had elected to opt for a white turtleneck sweater. Bobo bowed shyly as the crowd settled down in anticipation.

Brew busied himself with changing the reed on his horn and tried to blot out the image of Bobo leaping from the piano but there was nowhere to go. He rubbed his throat, tried to smile at Mary Ann as the sound check was completed. It was time.

They opened with one of Bobo's originals, simply titled 'Changes'. Bobo led off with a breathtaking solo introduction that dispelled any doubts about his return being genuine. Then, Deacon walked in, bass pulsing quietly, while Juice put the cymbals on simmer.

Brew decided that if he survived tonight, he'd just disappear. But now, locked into the music, his fingers flew over the horn in a blur while Deacon's throbbing bass and Juice's drums pushed and drove him through several choruses. Bobo, eyes closed, head back, nodded and passed the chords to Brew with love, till at last, Brew backed away and surrendered to Bobo.

Bobo spun out the old magic with a touch so deft he left the audience gasping for breath. This was the second coming of Bobo Jones. Rejuvenated and fresh lines flowed off his fingers effortlessly, transforming the mass of wood and metal and ivory into a total musical entity. Brew listened awestruck and nearly missed his entrance for the final cadenza.

He restated the plaintive theme, then made it his own, twisting, turning the melody before finally returning it safely to Bobo in its original form as the quartet came together for the final chord.

The applause that rang out and filled the room was deafening. But just as suddenly as it had erupted, it trailed off and lapsed into a tension-filled silence. Brew felt it then, his heart pounding, some murmuring as he caught a movement near the piano. He turned to see Bobo advancing towards him.

Brew stood frozen, staring hypnotically as Bobo stopped in front of him. As their eyes met in the hushed room, Bobo wiped away a tear, then suddenly grabbed Brew and hugged him close.

The audience began to clap again, only one or two people at first, gradually building in a crescendo, as Bobo whispered something in Brew's ear. No one heard what he'd said and it was later edited off the tape.

Brew wasn't sure he'd heard right at first. Bobo, face cracking into a huge grin, said it again. Brew smiled faintly, then threw his head back, laughing until tears came to his own eyes. Juice was laughing too and even Deacon smiled. Bobo went back to the piano and the rest of the evening went like a dream.

It was Mary Ann who finally remembered. Everyone was gone except for Manny who sat in a booth with them, calculating album sales and filling them in on the upcoming tour.

Brew sat slumped down while Mary Ann massaged his shoulders. The Newport people had been all smiles and had carted Bobo off to a celebration party. Brew had promised to join them later but for now he was content to bask in the luxurious feeling of freedom that washed over him in waves.

'What was it Bobo said to you? After the first number,' Mary Ann asked.

Brew grinned. 'Something I completely overlooked. "I knew all the time you wasn't Lee Evans, man," ' Brew said, imitating Bobo's hoarse whisper. ' "Lee was a brother and you sure don't look like a brother." '

Manny looked up puzzled, as Brew and Mary Ann both laughed. 'I don't get it,' he said. 'What's so funny about that?'

'Priorities, Manny. It's all a question of your priorities.'

A Rude Awakening

Avotcja

All the music is gone
It's gone
All the music is gone
All the music that I used to be
It's gone again
That old bitch life
Slapped me in the lip one more time
And snatched all the music
And left my heart soundless
The last note flew away
When my good old junkie buddy
Stuck his unmelodic gun in my face
And took my money & trust of people
And the last of my innocence died
With all the music
That's gone

I said the music is gone
All the music I used to be
It's gone, it flew away again
It's gone somewhere
With all the drunks and junkies
That just don't listen anymore
Because there's no more music left
That they can hear
In Scag-land
In pimp & pusherman Mad-land
In garbage can-land
It's gone . . . Lord

All the music
For a minute . . .
   . . . or two!

Seeing Her Off

Kitty Grime

Kitty Grime has been talking to jazz people since the year dot and has two books so far to show for it. This is her first piece of fiction (she's working on a novel) and it's for all the singers who told her a thing or two.

. . . ring ring . . . ring ring . . .

'Hello. Jasmin Dimmer speaking. Leonard and I aren't in at the moment. But please leave your name and number and we'll be in touch. Thanks for calling. Speak after the tone . . .'

. . . ring ring . . . ring ring . . .

'Hello, this is Felix Augener, well, to be truthful, it's not me, it's the old answering machine, but please don't ring off. Just leave your name and number and any message you like, and I'll be right back. Wait for the bleep . . .'

. . . ring ring . . . ring ring . . .

'Aug.'

'Ralph, my old son. All right for Friday, is it?'

'Look, I've just had a call from some bird trying to book me for Benny's . . .'

'Say no more. It'll be what's her name, Gennie something. Just been on to me.'

'Never heard of her.'

'One of these would-be singers. You must have seen her about. Little fat kid. Black hair. Teeth. Wears red. Always in front, wagging her bum, grinning away.'

'*That* one? Lovely little raver. Sings, does it?'

'Don't they all?'

'But what's all this about a Sunday at Benny's? With you and Dim?'

'Seems she gets Dim's number off somebody and phones him. Says she's a singer and she's got these tunes she wants sorting out. She's so keen, and Dim's soft, you know our young Leonard, so he has her round, doesn't he?'

'Any good?'

'He didn't say. So anyway, she only starts following us about. Every time I look up there she is. Comes over in the break, smiling, all that. Dim doesn't know where to look. So I say, "Oh, so you're a *singer*, how nice, well, stick around." And she only fucking *does*. And at the end she comes up and I say, "Oh, didn't realize you wanted to *sing*, shame, too late now, isn't it? Another time, right?" And the next week she's only there *again*. All night. So at the end she comes up and I say, "Oh, hello, didn't see you darling, sorry about that. Could have had a bit of a warble." And the *next* time I say, "Well, it's not too convenient, to be truthful, funny place, Benny doesn't relish singers, pity, not up to me, is it?" And the next time . . .'

'Won't give up, will she?'

'So I say to Dim, "Looks like this one really fancies you, you'll be all right there." Love to see him blush, young Dim. So to cut a long and boring story short, in the end I let her.'

'Sing?'

'Favour for a favour, darling, I tell her.'

'Enjoy yourself, did you?'

'Haven't had lipstick on my Y-fronts since I was on the road with Splurge.'

'Well, well, well . . .'

'So she has her little sing. And, fuck me, up comes Benny at the finish and says, "Who was *that*?" And next thing, she's only on the blower saying he's offered her one of his Sunday nights.'

'Well, what's it like, anyway? The singing, I mean?'

'Look, if it'd been bad, I'd have noticed.'

. . . ring ring . . . ring ring . . .

'Eve? It's Gennie.'

'*Lovie*, how nice to hear from you. What have you been doing with yourself? Still singing?'

'Eve, I've done it, finally done it, finally finally finally . . .'

'What, for heaven's sake?'

'Benny's booked me. Benny's finally booked me.'

'Oh, you had me worried for a moment, Gen. Well, that's good. What can I say? I knew you'd do it in the end. All these months. Or is it years? I'm losing track.'

'Not been easy, has it? Just getting him to hear me.'

'I tell you what, we'll all come down and cheer.'

'Oh, Eve, I just had to tell you. I was just bursting to tell someone. There's so much to do, all the music to sort out. You know, I've been planning it all for ages, lying awake all night, singing it all to myself. You know, really nice things, unusual, you know. Amazing how it happened, really. I was just sitting in with Dim and Aug, fantastic players, you know, the *best*, oh it makes such a difference. And Benny comes up and says, "That's just what the group needed." So I'm going to book them. And then I thought of Ral, fantastic saxophone player. It'll sound so *good*. Oh, Eve, I just can't stop jumping up and down and going "Wheeee", you know me.'

'Up and down all the time, aren't you lovie? But I think it's great, really great. And about time, too.'

'So, I'll be in touch, Eve.'

'Fingers crossed, lovie. Gonna go in there a nobody and come out a star, aren't you?'

'Hopefully. See you, Eve.'

. . . ring ring . . . ring ring . . .

'Dim, it's Aug. Been on to you, then, has she?'

'Sorry?'

'Little Miss Ever Ready?'

'Oh yes, her.'

'Doing it, then, are we? Should be a laugh.'

'What's it worth, anyway? Benny's usual?'

'Pitiful, really. But Nelson's always helps, doesn't it? I'll tell her, "Yes" then? How do you feel?'

'Just don't let her rabbit your ear off. I know she's keen and all that, but . . .'

'Too fucking keen, that's her problem. Right, young Leonard, it's on then. See you Friday.'

'Good, last week, wasn't it?'

'Enjoyed it.'

. . . ring ring . . . ring ring . . .

'Dim.'

'Oh hello Ral.'

'Doing this Sunday thing, then?'

'Aug was saying she's trying to lumber you as well.'

'On, then, is it? Thought I'd better check. She sounds a bit of a nutter.'

'Talked us into it.'

'I only do jazz gigs these days.'

'Supposed to be jazz, isn't it?'

'Well, it won't be if she's singing all night. I only like them if they sing what I want to play.'

'Right. No problem.'

'Well, Dim, always a pleasure, you and Aug, you know that. Nice. Oh, regards to Min. How is she, these days?'

'Don't see too much of her, do I?'

'Still got the job, then?'

'Thank Christ.'

'Wish mine'd get off her lovely little backside. See you Friday, all right?'

'Looking forward to it.'

'Take care.'

. . . *ring ring* . . . *ring ring* . . .

'Min, it's Maj.'

'Maj, it's been ages.'

'I know, aren't I awful?'

'All go, isn't it? Look, I'm just on my way out to the . . .'

'Min, who the hell's this bird that's on the phone to Aug all the time? It's really getting on my tits. Gennie something.'

'Oh, yes, the one who thinks she can sing.'

'Never heard of her.'

'Leonard had her round one afternoon. I come in with the shopping, there they are, heads together. Picking his brains, he says. So I tell him, "I don't want her round here again unless she's *paying* you." '

'Aug says she's too fucking keen, that's her trouble. Can she sing?'

'Leonard says she's got a good ear.'

'Aug says she's fat and sexy.'

'What's he trying to do? Wind you up or something?'

'Highly likely. I'm off him at the moment, as it happens. Who's she with, anyway?'

'Leonard says she's a bit of a les, must be.'

'Well, don't tell Aug. He loves all that, birds together, always gets him going.'

'Anyway, it now appears she has this gig. All these great players scratching about for a living, and some young singer just walks in there and . . .'

'Now watch it, watch it, *I* sing. Remember? I know it's been a while, but . . .'

'Maj, look, I'm late as it is, must love and leave you . . .'

'Right, Min, see you. Rumour has it she's sitting in with them on Friday. Fancy going?'

'Leonard hates me going on his gigs, really. Says I always give him a hard time on the way home . . .'

'Aug says I always get pissed. What else can you do? Tell you what, I'll blag them into letting me do a number. Just like the old days. Oh, come on, Min, it'll be a giggle. And watch me wipe the floor with little Miss Fat Arse.'

'Let me see what he says, Maj, must go.'

'You tell your young Leonard from me he owes you a night out. See you Friday.'

. . . *ring ring* . . . *ring ring* . . .

'Hello.'

'Hello, Gennie, this is your friendly neighbourhood rapist.'

'Aug. That's not funny, you know.'

'Oh, shut up, you know you love it. Well, young Gennie, sorted out the Norwegians, then, have you?'

'The what?'

'Fjords, chords, my darling. Chords, *chords*, know what I mean?'

'Well . . . '

'*Well?* Well, you better get it together, darling, sharpish. There won't be time for any of your messing about on Sunday.'

'Messing about?'

'Sorting your keys out, all that. You're not sitting-in in your pub on the corner now, you know.'

'Don't worry, Aug, I'm . . .'

'*I'm* not worrying, it's supposed to be *your* gig, darling. Still on, by the way, is it?'

'Of course it's still on, at least when I spoke to Benny about the . . .'

'Look, I just happen to go back years, darling, years and years. Do us all a great big favour, and just don't try to get too clever, that's all. None of your shoobeedoos. Just sing the song. Let *us* do the jazz.'

'But . . .'

'Stick to something you know. Something we all know.'

'But I've been working on all these great songs. Months, it's been. I *told* you, and . . .'

'Don't wet yourself, darling. Just trying to help you, that's all.'

'Should I talk to Dim, do you think? I know he's a bit busy, but . . .'

'That's right, you talk to Dim.'

. . . *ring ring* . . . *ring ring* . . .

'Yes?'

'Dim.'

'Oh hello, Aug.'

'On to you just now, was she? Moaning?'

'Afraid so.'

'I've just been telling her, "Do yourself a favour, none of your fucking obscurities." '

'Min told her I was busy. Now she's going on about sending me tapes of all these songs she says she wants to do. It's only a gig, for Christ's sake . . .'

'Getting boring, isn't it? Not enjoying this, are we? I'll have to tell her.'

'Thanks, Aug.'

. . . *ring ring* . . . *ring ring* . . .

'Oh, Eve, it's Gennie again.'

'How's it all going, lovie? Who's persecuting you this time?'

'Eve, I'm in despair.'

'You're always in despair, aren't you? Gennie, it'll be all right tomorrow, I'm sure. Should be quite a crowd. I've been making all the right phone calls.'

'I'm getting scared. I never used to be scared.'

'Deep breaths, lovie. And be sure to wear your red thing.'

'It's all I've got. Makes me look fat, though.'

'It makes you look fantastic. Who's been telling you you're fat, for heaven's sake?'

'I'm sorry about all this, Eve, it's just nerves, I suppose. Can't seem to do anything right at all.'

'It's supposed to be a man's world, jazz, isn't it? All right, you're a woman. All right, you're a singer. Make 'em have it, as they say.'

'Just had Aug on the phone saying, "We don't want to . . ." '

'Whose gig is it?'

. . . *ring ring* . . . *ring ring* . . .

'Hello, it's Gennie. Sorry, can I speak to Dim? Only a moment. About tomorrow?'

'He's in the bath.'

. . . *ring ring* . . . *ring ring* . . .

'Hello.'

'Hello? Mrs Augener?'

'Who else? Look, Gennie, Aug's just popped out for a moment, sorry and all that . . .'

'How did you know it was me?'

'I've got a good ear too, you know.'

. . . ring ring . . . ring ring . . .
'Hello. Jasmin Dimmer speaking. Leonard and I aren't in at the moment. But please leave your name and number . . .'

. . . ring ring . . . ring ring . . .
'Hello, this is Felix Augener, well, to be truthful, it's not me, it's the old answering machine . . .'

. . . ring ring . . . ring ring . . .
'Ral, it's Gennie. Sorry, but I just wanted to, that is, like, check, I just have to have a word with *somebody* about what we're going to do tomorrow, you know I'd been planning all these . . .'
'It's not too convenient right now, know what I mean? Talk to you at the gig, right?'

. . . ring ring . . . ring ring . . . ring ring . . . ring ring . . . ring ring . . . ring ring . . . ring ring . . . ring ring . . .

. . . ring ring . . . ring ring . . .
'I'd like to speak to Felix Augener, please.'
'Speaking.'
'I don't suppose you'll remember me, but it's Eve Lesser. I'm a friend of Gennie's. The singer?'
'Oh yes?'
'I was at the gig last Sunday.'
'I remember.'
'I know it sounds a bit funny, but have you heard from her? I mean, Gennie? Since the gig?'
'Never a dickie bird.'
'Well, I've been ringing and ringing her number all week. No reply. It's a bit odd, somehow.'
'Oh really?'
'And I've just seen that bit in the paper this morning.'
'Oh, that.'
'Wondered if she'd seen it. I thought it might cheer her up a bit, silly girl. You know, I found her down in the Ladies after the gig, crying her little heart out.'
'You're joking. Look, I'm a bit busy right now . . .'
'I thought you'd be in touch with her, that's all. Well, I'll keep trying.'

. . . ring ring . . . ring ring . . .

'Min? Is Dim about?'

'Hello, Maj. Sorry, he's having a bit of a lie-in. Didn't get in till five.'

'Did you see it? That write-up this morning?'

'What? What write-up?'

'Just you listen to this. "And featured on three all-too-short numbers was a real find. A bright-eyed young thing, whose energy and jazz feel could help lift the group out of its, quote, worthy instrumentalist, unquote, doldrums." And wait, it goes on, "Gennie . . ." '

'Anything about the music?'

'Of course not. Fucking *critics*.'

'Aug must be highly delighted.'

'He's *seething*.'

. . . *ring ring* . . . *ring ring* . . .

'Aug.'

'Ral. All right for Friday, is it?'

'Pick me up, same place?'

'Right. Should be a good one.'

'Looking forward to it.'

'Oh, Ral, by the way, better warn you, Maj'll be with us, sorry about that. Got herself all excited about singing again. I thought we'd finally heard the last of it, but . . .'

'Good thing about mine, she doesn't pretend to know a thing about music, lovely little darling.'

'Got to keep them happy, though, these wives, know what I mean?'

'Talking of singers . . . shock, really, about what's her name.'

'Young Gennie? Yes, bit of a shock.'

'Not nice, going under a car like that, right after the gig. Pissed, was she?'

'Pure accident, has to be.'

'I'd heard she was in one of these comas all week and nobody knew who it was. Nothing to go on. Nothing in her bag but bits of music.'

'You remember that friend of hers? The old boiler who was at the gig?'

'The one who wanted us all to go back to her place?'

'Eve, is it? Anyway, it seems she's organizing something. Wanted us to play. No money, of course. Can't see myself making it somehow. Maj is none too keen, hates funerals.'

'Strikes me as a right old liberty, Aug, all things considered.'

'Not as if anybody *knew* her, is it?'

Touching the Past

Robert Sargent

Uptown New Orleans, 1940,
And here was a man of the right colour,
Old enough to have been there,

Who maybe heard. So I inquired
From the old man doing his yard work,
'Ever hear Buddy Bolden play?'

'Ah me,' he said, stopping his work,
'Yes. But you mean *King, King* Bolden.
That's what we called him then.'

He leaned on his rake a while, resting.
'Used to play in Algiers, played so loud ﹣
We could hear him clear 'cross the river.'

He seemed listening. 'King Bolden, now,
There was a man could play.' We stood there,
Thinking about it, smiling.

From: *Aspects of a Southern Story*, The Word Works, 1983

Listen!!!

Avotcja

Musicians
  Dying
    Crying
      Getting squashed
Drowning in wine bottles – and hot shots
Instant heaven
  In constant hell
The funky Apple trying to bury all of us
In Lady Scag
Happiness is the next E-flat
Til some chump tries to lay his secretary
At the top of his lungs
In the middle of your best solo
Musicians
  Screaming
    Starving
      Leaving
Their axe
For a gig as a waitress at the corner candy store
Or a job as a bus boy at Horn & Hardarts
Children got to eat
And ain't nobody listening but the bar maid
When she ain't beating off the drunks

Musicians
Trying to get away from – the entertainment freaks
Who can't hear
   Unless you shake your feet
      And dance a little
Or let your left breast
Hang over the top of your evening gown
And pant a little in the microphone
& we cry
   & we die
      & so will the music, if no one listens
Listen? – Listen!! You better listen!!!
Before there's no more music left for you to hear!!!!!

The Devil and All that Jazz

Robert J. Tilley

Robert Tilley was born in Yorkshire and raised in the West Country. He has been writing sporadically since the 1950s, mostly for science fiction and fantasy magazines. A graphic designer and lecturer until his recent retirement, he plays the tenor saxophone and the clarinet.

World War II closed out a real bust from Satan's angle, so he decided to go guerrilla again while he scored a new book for Korea and a few other gigs.

It wasn't long after that that a devil camouflaged in a drape suit and carrying a trumpet case under its arm swaggered into the Blue Box just as the six-piece band stomped off into a fresh set.

It listened critically, clucking loudly at intervals. The set finished to a mild spatter of applause and the musicians retired backstage to finish off a private bottle.

All except the trumpet player, that is. To his considerable surprise he found himself sitting on a bar stool while somebody breathed sulphurously in his ear.

'Man, you were really terrible,' the devil said, meaning awful.

The trumpet player thanked him, and ordered gin.

The devil scowled uncertainly, then continued its insidious onslaught.

'I mean, but terrible,' it said, offensively. 'I've heard some bum trumpet in my time, but you're one step down from nothing. An A-plus drag.'

The trumpet player suggested a few minutes' brisk exercise in the alley.

The devil cackled. 'Stow it, stupid. I might bust your lip. Besides, I'm here to do you a favour.'

'Favour, schmavour,' said the trumpet player. 'Blow.'

'Delighted, I'm sure,' said the devil. It smirked conceitedly and patted its trumpet case. 'Mind if I sit in on the next set? You could do with a pointer or two. Or maybe three.'

'So help me, you're some top-heavy guy, all right,' said the trumpet player. 'Who do you think you are, Gabriel?'

The devil winced painfully at this obscenity, then recovered its aplomb. It sneered. 'What's with you? Chicken?'

The trumpet player sneered back and jerked his head to where the rest of the band were drifting back on to the stand.

'She's all yours, hot-shot. Let's hear what a real live genius can do.'

The devil unpacked his trumpet, sprang on to the stand and blasted its way through sixteen searing choruses of 'Who's Sorry Now', finishing on a magnificently full-toned G above top C. Eight glasses broke on a shelf behind the bar. The applause was thunderous.

It rejoined the trumpet player, preening itself. The trumpet player looked respectfully despondent.

'Man, what have you got for a lip?' he queried. 'Asbestos? Where'd you learn to blow that much horn?'

'In a joint where they play it *real* hot,' said the devil. It leaned forward confidingly. 'So tell me, how would *you* like to be able to wail like that?'

'Man,' said the trumpet player, 'oh, man.' He looked even more despondent.

'For a small fee,' said the devil, smiling evilly, 'it could be arranged.'

The trumpet player looked incredulous. 'Yeah? Like how much?'

'Your soul.'

'Man, what kind of jazz is that?' asked the trumpet player plaintively. 'What are you, some kind of pusher?'

The devil introduced itself, and explained.

The trumpet player looked even more incredulous, but thoughtful. 'You mean I get to blow like that if I jack in my soul when I cut out?'

'On the button,' said the devil. It cocked a satanic eyebrow. 'Well, how about it? Deal?'

The trumpet player licked his lips greedily. 'Maybe. But I don't want no fast shuffle. How long have I got before I do kick?'

The devil put on horn-rimmed executive-type glasses and studied a notebook.

'Another forty-eight years, seven months, two weeks, four days, six hours, three minutes and thirty seconds, as from – ' it studied its

wristlet, carefully ' – now.'

The trumpet player synchronized his watch with the devil's.

'OK. Deal. Well, I'll see you around.'

He leaped back on to the stand, grabbed his trumpet, and led the band into a breakneck 'After You've Gone', during the course of which a further fourteen glasses shattered behind the bar. The customers went wild and the manager raised his pay twenty dollars a week, minus deductions for broken glassware.

The devil left, leering a triumphant leer.

A few years later, the devil, checking out its investment, so to speak, dropped in at a joint in Chi where the trumpet player was billed. Muted sounds greeted it from the bandstand where the trumpet player was ensconced with a tenor and three rhythm. The devil reached the bar just as the trumpet player left the stand while the tenor worked through something solo.

'Well,' said the devil jovially, 'how's the boy?'

'Oh,' said the trumpet player. 'Hi.' He shrugged. 'Y'know?'

'That so?' said the devil. It studied the customers approvingly. 'Good house tonight. All waiting to hear you cut loose with some of that real wild sound, I bet you.' It cocked an eye at the trumpet player. 'Say, that was kind of pussyfoot stuff you were pushing out just now. What gives? Sore lip?'

'Huh?' said the trumpet player. 'Oh. Nah, the lip's great. Don't blow that way no more, is all.'

'Huh?' said the devil in turn.

'Blowin' cool now, man,' said the trumpet player. 'Don't dig that Dixie-type sound no more. Dig Chet, Lee and those cats. Y'know?'

The devil blanched. 'You mean – ?'

'Yay,' said the trumpet player. He studied the devil's rapidly paling features. 'What's with you, man? You look kinda – oh, I get it. You cats don't dig the sound down in your pad, huh?'

The devil shook its head numbly.

'Plays hell with the climate,' it muttered through chattering fangs. 'Big flu epidemic last year. Some flute player. Even the Chief got a touch. Temperature went down to two hundred and something – look.' It licked blue lips, pleadingly. 'Couldn't you kind of switch back? I mean – '

'Well, hell, man,' said the trumpet player. 'Sure like to help out, an' all, but that's the way it comes now. Y'know? Like, think cool.' He looked vaguely embarrassed. 'Strictly for the schnooks, that Dixie. Y'know?'

The devil nodded feebly.

B Flat, Bebop, Scat

'Well,' said the trumpet player apologetically. 'That's how it goes, I guess. Life, and all that jazz.' He ordered Scotch and turned his attention back to the stand, where the tenor was worming blandly through its fourth chorus of 'Cool Breeze'. 'Great, Dad. Go.'

The devil, hacking abominably, went, and it didn't come back, either.

Ellington, Duke of Washington

Campbell Burnap

You might have passed, unknown,
Decades ago.
Tuberculated
In a meagre mini-cask . . . anonymous.
An incidental pin-prick event
Like one droplet of salty rain
Unnoticed
That joins up and swills
Briefly and inevitably
To the drain darkness.
Only your mother might have cried
And a lonely aunt in a far-off town.

Instead? . . .
These wreaths bear every flag and tongue.

You were the raindrop
That splashed
And arced away, glinting
To fall alone on a flat petal of passion –
The Creation Flower.
I think you listened
Beneath an oblique and tropic
Polar tree
Jungle edge
To the wind's beige cooing
Bringing exotic rhythms on magenta haze
Smeared with indigo moods,
With tawny tones and rainbow chords.

B Flat, Bebop, Scat

I think you heard,
Must have heard and must have seen
Those slender coffee-curving spines
And thighs
Which drifted, dancing slowly from the shadows
Bringing secret quaver-codes
That only you could understand.

We'll miss you, Voice of America.

Today, with grace and winning husky charm
You called the final number.
The last set.
The infinite intermission.

Excuse me . . . Do you still take requests?
When it's *our* turn to come
May we have a seat near the band?
Will you still love us madly?
How shall we find you?
Is there a *train* we can take?

Correspondence

Alice Wooledge Salmon

Alice Wooledge Salmon, who lives in London, is a native of New York and a graduate of Vassar. She has the dual profession of writer and photographer, broadcasts for the BBC, and has been a chef at London's Ma Cuisine restaurant and the Connaught Hotel. Her work, on a variety of subjects, appears regularly in British and American magazines, and she won the Glenfiddich Food Writer of the Year award for 1982 and for 1984. She is co-author of The Wine and Food Society Menu Book *and a contributor to* Christie's Wine Companion 2.

> Où est le Christophe Colomb à qui l'on devra l'oubli d'un continent?
>
> Apollinaire, 'Toujours'

For a long year, Martha and Louis Cinnabar had lived in Los Angeles and were now en route to London and home. Home in a sense, because habitually they travelled and lingered all over the globe in pursuit of respective careers. It was Louis's as conductor which had sent them to LA and that city which Martha found so tedious as practically to numb her vocation as writer.

A big hairy sprawl of fully equipped banality was how she saw Hollywood's Center for the Performing Arts – where Louis was conducting – the guests at innumerable parties, their relentless houses, and almost anywhere she could drive or phone from the rented metres of glass and stilts along which the pair of them teetered. A novel that Martha had begun on the Suffolk coast and advanced in London had choked and spluttered through southern California, which Louis called 'a foretaste of hell' and from whose broadcast they flew, buoyant as light aircraft, as soon as his contracts permitted.

They landed on the Caribbean island of Santa Rosa, on a spree, stripping off the dry and deadly LA heat for high humidity and the promise of banana trees, hibiscus. Temperatures were way up but relieved by breeze; they checked into a tower pitched beside the Atlantic and could feel the ocean's muscle.

They found that Santa Rosa, billed as trivial, has been taking issue. Their hotel filled one end of a long, tall strip for heedless tourists – the kind with money so new that it rubs and pinches in all directions – and well below the terrace of their bedroom a spit of land led to ruins of a Spanish fort, one of many that formerly protected the old city of Descansado. All the others have been rebuilt, shined up and woven tight with tourist weft, but this fort had sea grapes growing from fragmented walls and an attendant swell of tide that was getting the better of several edges.

Such intriguing neglect drew Louis and Martha – dedicated walkers immune to jogging – away from The Strip, past the fort to the part of town where English is a rare sound. Santa Rosa has long been free of Spain, depends unofficially on the USA and its capacity for rum, coffee, tobacco, and the absorption of poor immigrants in return for unlimited supplies of ten-day visitors. Louis and Martha met none of these in the newer parts of Descansado. The Strip makes the border, the gaudy hem to the old, now tourist-tinselled city, where plastic sandals and English are commonplace among candy-pretty houses and flame trees that drip in the rain; the modern streets keep to different rhythms.

'Such heat,' said Louis at noon, tearing off his sweat-soaked hat. 'I've never been in a Latin country where people don't stop for *la siesta*.' Here, no one seemed exactly to stop; at the height of the sun they slowed from what was already a sedate pace to a sort of loll, brought more *chinas* – the sweet orange stripped of its zest and sucked for juice – from street vendors, but kept on selling rather florid goods in the shops, answering office telephones, and hanging around outside the high schools. That American influence.

The Cinnabars walked frequently in spite of heat, and liked seeing large families with small children who took to the streets, late afternoon and all day Saturday. The children had the docile, jelly-baby look of Latin infants, jelly babies kitted out in starched pastels below solemn cheeks and well-brushed liquorice mops.

'Look here,' said Martha, peering into windows-ful of photo-

43

graphers' work in colour. There were large 'portraits' of fiancées, brides, mothers, grandmothers, children – all as expected. What had caught her attention were several shots of women, dressed like the brides in floor-length white, but fully pregnant. There was a haze round the edge of each print – vaseline smeared on the camera lens – and always, the husband had an ear pressed against the woman's belly, while he, any onlooking children, and the wife in question wore smiles of the blessed.

'I like this place,' said Martha, taking Louis's hand; 'I haven't felt so pleased about things for ages.' Louis was a generation or so her senior, had divorced his earlier wife to marry her and become so much a part of Martha, so much her root and branch that when they were constantly together she was almost unaware of him, as you would not think much about an arm or ear. They were often separated by exactions of work, which she accepted cheerfully but with the discomfort of one who's misplaced her specs, and when eventually she heard his slam of the door, his shout as she let herself in, she lit the skies with a blaze of pleasure.

'You're a Cinnabar-innocent.'

'I know,' said Louis. They sat toying with concoctions, plus or minus rum – they were too hot to care – in a dusty café, sparring partners. They liked plays on words, neologisms, mnemonics, 'Le Buisson du Berger' for Shepherd's Bush, verbal gymnastics in a language by now fairly private and almost always ready to dance.

'You're pretty innocent,' he went on. 'When you said that man's paintings were terrible, you must have known he was standing three feet away from you.'

'He wasn't. And anyway he didn't hear me. And even if he did, so what? They *are* terrible; maybe now they'll get better.'

'You're shameless.'

'Yes.'

'And you surprise me. I thought you liked eggs, paintings of eggs?'

'Eggs yes, but not something rotten.'

' "Surprise". Always reminds me of that grammarian, the Frenchman, Littré, in bed with the maid when his wife walks in. "Monsieur, I'm surprised!" says the wife, and Littré corrects her: "No, Madame, *you* are astonished; *we* are surprised." '

And on and on like this, both worse and better. Martha liked men with guts – was a gutsy woman – men who took risks, Louis who told her within three days of meeting that he loved her, that she was *exactly* what he'd 'dreamed about', to which she said of course, 'You must be nuts!' while thinking in fact, 'He's rather nice'; an older man (her decided preference) – a *very* nice man as well as a brave one.

'Y'know, I'm whacked,' said the brave man. 'Hasn't this year been a slog!' He shook a little tenseness round the shoulders and rubbed his eyes, a bright, quick blue undimmed by Santa Rosan ultraviolet. 'Let's stay here a while, drive up to the hills, see what's happening.'

So they did that, rented a wide, rather old but air-conditioned car and drove, like Santa Rosans, at a leisured rate out of Descansado along country roads past fields of cane and grey-blue pineapples, up into foothills where men and boys hailed them from stalls at the verge. They stopped, chose whole coconuts from the depths of elderly Frigidaires, had the tops lopped away with machetes, took up straws and drew deep on the blandly soothing coconut 'water'. One of the men, speaking English, asked if they wanted the water 'at normal weather; either way is good for the kidneys'.

They drove on towards mountains – what Santa Rosans call the *cordillera* – into thick foliage, a true jungle of flowering trees, the large-leaved plantains and bananas, frequent waterfalls. They stayed at a green-and-white inn among red hibiscus, formerly part of a coffee plantation; a house with wide verandas and very plain, clean bedrooms where fans slowly moved the air as Louis kissed Martha in ways she thought he'd forgotten. His nose, just barely Roman – no more than the break in the trousers of the late Duke of Windsor – had always impressed her. His aromas didn't cloy.

'You're a dangerous woman,' he whispered; his eyes creased and crinkled, teasing as usual.

'You betcha,' growled Martha, holding him dearly. Tree frogs sang through the night.

In a sense he bored her. His mind lacked shady places, big comfortable plane trees or rocky outcrops under which to lie back, take stock. Though wrapped up in music, he saw it as an adversary, a beloved opponent to be bested at every performance; Baker once more confronting his sources of the Nile. Louis was an extrovert, Martha was absorbent, spread things out inside. But there was a joy about her husband, headwaters unsullied by life's dark troubles which, coupled with his kindness, his nimble wit, suited Martha and assured her that boredom could have its precious depths.

Walking in the forest round the hacienda they rediscovered silence; not, certainly, absence of noise, nor the gingerly pull of constraint. Silence of the random thought that fades, fosters another, shakes out a spread of impulse. Some of the sparks catch fire. Then the hush of achievement, between movements, the pause that serves as reply. Silence that the inexperienced, seeing a couple mutely dining out, can take for negligence.

Louis had been seeking information, opened relevant books and grazed among them. He did not like to be interrupted and did this well before Martha, no early riser, was even *compos*. They wandered, after breakfast, sat through the sudden evenings sipping drinks on the veranda and discussed his finds.

'Apparently,' said Louis, 'these Caribbean islands are the peaks of drowned mountains, an extension of the Andes. They're immensely high. Higher even than the Himalayas, if you measure right from the sea's bed.'

'Drowning mountains.' Martha imagined the terrifying process, the notion of extreme heights and depths, apocalyptic peril.

'It's just not in keeping.' She gestured round her. 'For *this* peak, anyhow. It's like a pet, a domestic animal – at most a cow, a goat – in comparison with *that*.'

They sipped, steeped in wellbeing and the pleasures of danger felt from considerable distance. Tree frogs were up in the dark forest.

'And there's something else. Columbus is reckoned to be buried in Santo Domingo. There's a cathedral there, with a bronze coffin, and inside are meant to be Christopher's bones.'

'Christopher's bones! I've never even thought about them,' said Martha, surprised.

'Well, I always imagined they would be in Spain, if anywhere, if not bleached on some sea coast. But apparently it's his brother who's lying in Seville, and he, well he's just across the water on another of your drowning peaks.'

A bar near the hacienda ran a juke box with American records, old and scratched; they could hear rusty snatches of 'How High the Moon', mercifully faint. Martha rested her head on Louis's arm.

'Isn't it strange to think of us, and him, with millions of others, dead and alive, all over these islands, and most of us – would you say clinging to the wreckage? Most of us so *ignorant* except perhaps Columbus, who sought.'

'I hope you'll start to search again,' he said. 'That book of yours, now we've left the City of the Angels.' He went on talking, quietly making a space round the two of them. He had long, capable hands, wore the narrowest of wedding-rings, slightly loose; as Martha would hold him, so Louis held Martha.

Back again in their tower-by-the-sea, they watched the fort below become less and less of a picture postcard; it was linked to ponderous Spanish plazas with their marzipan churches and clipped fig trees of Santa Rosan coastal towns, to cactus fences down rural beaches, to the *chinas* and photographs of the pregnant women. They went at all hours on to their balcony, suspended like a basket above the Atlantic, sat reading and observing as the ocean blew up constant balloons of African cloud from the north and east, perpetually forming, dispersing, often shedding a quick shock of rain. The Caribbean, round the island's other side, is a deep and voluptuous blue, a tropical colour with only a flash of the poison green that intimates shipwreck and buried treasure; the Atlantic, they found, though habitually calm, is close to menace, the grey water dribbled with gold but the shipwrecks austere suggestions of Breton seamen dashed against rocks, submarines lost with all hands. The early sun lit twelve, fourteen, twenty storeys of slight variation in one façade that looped for miles along The Strip, lit it for the profit of other elements, crouching, powerful, always in wait. At night, Martha and Louis lay with the door to their balcony open wide, heard the sea's pitch through discreet air conditioning as they woke and slept.

They noticed a district between The Strip and the modern heart of the new town with its back streets of rusting cars and hot little dwellings scarcely feeling the heaving efforts of tinny air coolers. This region between was like a 1930s Hollywood of slightly resorty, slightly suburban addresses in pink or white stucco with rippling red roofs. Some of the houses had stained glass and elaborately grilled verandas, most dangled names like Miramar, Caledonia, La Concha, El Palomar – the latter a stack of small apartments near the shore, a turreted, very artful dovecote at one corner, hibiscus cascading from white balconies, a garden of overgrown palms. It was luxuriant with – fable? decadence? a vision of Palm Beach some fifty years earlier?

'It says "for Rent",' Louis observed when they'd been passing El Palomar, off and on, for ten days; a much-tried sign made public, in English, 'Apt-kitch'ette for Rent'. What tourist would postpone his return to New York, New Jersey, or Philadelphia, what engineer down from Chicago on a few months' contract would pass up hotel comforts – even those from across the road – in order to rent whatever was offered?

It was Martha, on impulse, who took this flat. Louis was called by his agent; could he *please* fly off to Tokyo – emergency – illness – eleventh-hour replacement – six weeks with the Tokyo Philharmonic – huge fee and everyone desperate?

'Go,' said Martha. 'I guess you just about have time, and I'd really like to stay. I think I can get things moving with that book again.'

So Louis went to Tokyo, and what had started as a few weeks' departure was extended, for Martha, into a great, shady, roomy space where in no spirit of contradiction the sun beat down and tropical rain drove into the sea. She slept late among the shabby furniture and curious tenants of El Palomar. One of these could speak four or five languages, another kept three dogs and sent them nightly through hoops in a club on The Strip, a third – an American – played his trumpet at a dive for jazz across the way. Out came the book and

Martha examined, revised, and cogitated, reflecting for stretches on Roy Russell, whose letters from London had begun to arrive. Martha had met Louis while involved with Roy and this involvement had never ceased.

To Roy she had come years before, like a pirate, nonchalant, for pillage, and with surprise known the most achingly perfect heartlands of mystery; 'pleasures which are lightly called physical', as Colette wrote and those who are lucky discover, with wonder. Roy too was a writer, very pressed by humble birth (he had started life as 'Ron'), a couple of wives, the need to sustain the usual necessities and to express what everything else left so little time for. So his books were rare but sinewed, having fought for life against other matters, and his letters to Martha were often abundant. During the first months of their affair, she'd been amazed by the notes, postcards, poems, and sometimes two, three pages at once with which Roy pursued her. Other men had written to Martha, of course, but never so often and deftly, and she was delighted, rushed downstairs to the morning post, looked forward to arrival home and unexpected hand deliveries. It was thrilling, a romp conducted on special terrain carved from two lives during one prolonged autumn.

Then there were troubles, they stopped meeting, and Martha, who couldn't think how to do without him, cried, 'How will I live without all those letters?' The details of loss can be harder to bear than the absence. These were dark days, though always resolute – Martha didn't believe in collapse – and just when they were lightening, Roy began to write again, guardedly, the way you would eat after long fast or illness. At the same time she encountered wonderful, enveloping Louis, about whom there was no question that here was the man for every day, for as long as possible, for ever. And the funny thing was that Louis too sent letters, large well-spaced syllables linked with flourish, had dropped them off 'By hand', mailed them rat-tat-tat from all sorts of far-flung places.

Eventually Martha had married Louis while keeping Roy, his letters – sporadic or frequent – their rare but mythic meetings that were fired always with the melancholy sun of that long first autumn. Could so much emotion, addiction simply vanish? At either end of a lean rope, seldom taut, they held something determined.

In LA, Roy's letters – which came often, at Martha's request – had entertained her, buoyed her mind that wandered compulsively from almost any other form of written page. As they didn't meet that year, Martha was able to imagine their rapport was turning, with ease, into friendship; probably as well, she would think, until a phrase of Roy's tight, methodical script, marked with literary allusion, coiled intentionally round her – soft, importunate as velvet, skin, the scent of a ripe and uncut peach, the brutality of memory.

When Martha sank temporary stakes at El Palomar, she wrote her change of plan to Roy, who answered swiftly and with much amusement; Louis, on reaching Tokyo, sent daily letters or three words on a postcard, as was his custom. Roy's envelopes were addressed to 'Martha Cinnabar', never to 'Mrs . . .' nor, heaven forbid, to 'Ms . . .'. Louis wrote 'Mrs Martha [or 'Louis'] Cinnabar', or simply 'Mrs Cinnabar'. This variety caused her to speculate; Louis was of an earlier generation which could not be imagined putting the stark and almost defiant 'Martha Cinnabar', yet plain 'Mrs Cinnabar' sounded quaint, so prim, like addressing Matron. Or could it imply 'The One, The Only'? Or merely that Louis, as ever, wrote in a hurry. Roy's unembellished 'Martha Cinnabar' was satisfactory; his good instincts rejected the 'Ms', the limbless 'Mrs M. [Or 'L.'] Cinnabar' for a couple of words sent out on their own, with conviction.

The coupled words came pasted one day to an envelope wrapping a jazz tape which Roy had compiled from various sources; music they'd listened to, mainly. The syrupy tremolo of saxophone, the love-wounded, liquor-sodden torchiness of trumpet, the pyramids built and demolished by a lone piano, all were there, like the concentrated fruit of so much passion and profuse emotion. It floored her to hear this, and the sudden, insistent pressure, like hands compressing tense and painful muscles, was both well-nigh unbearable and a relief, if terrible. She turned up the volume and let the music scream.

Was it days later she began, as it were, to miss her specs? Martha needed Louis, always, his gift of independence, the vulnerability that shaped his assurance and made her want to shield him from any spring of pain, while the only person who could see her through distress, avowed or unspoken, was Louis. There were times when she wanted to run, but always towards him, not away, and rarely with the wish to confide, almost never to confess, but to feel the race of sap through their mutual tree; the secret strength of marriage.

As she grappled in thought and cradled her past and might-have-beens like a recovered child, seated cross-legged on the frayed carpet, wondering why Roy had sent the tape – and where *was* Louis? – and why he'd sent it *now*, like a fist that opened to clutch her throat, sweaty not with aftermath but with heat from this odd and lovable island, in the midst of all this there came an abrupt knock and Martha went to answer.

'I can hear you like jazz.' The tape had run, loud, through many sets of batteries but not, so far, into any complaints.

'Come across tonight and hear us play.'

B Flat, Bebop, Scat

It was Frankie, the American trumpeter who lived upstairs.

'About nine, nine thirty. I'll see you have a table up front, and I'll tell the boss to make sure no one bothers you. Unless you wanna be bothered?'

'Yes, tell him that,' said Martha. 'OK, I'll be there.'

Frankie seemed a pleasant, forty-ish fellow, looking amiably slobby and quite unhealthy, like many white musicians. Martha was glad to be distracted from her round of ragged abrasions and to enter, with purpose, the Hotel Playa across the road, whose basement sheltered Frankie's jazz club. The Playa was old, by Santa Rosan standards, low, with the peachy stucco and undulating roof of the quarter surrounding, and had fallen further, from higher, than El dear-old Palomar. The lobby seemed braced by huge marble lamps, bone-pale, with moony alabaster globes and dark flexes that scuttled away beneath carpets. Ten-ton white elephants, worth a fortune to someone who would doubtless never see them. Along the walls were enlarged photos, black and white, of what Martha supposed had been members of Santa Rosan society, 'le tout-Santa Rosa', in the 1930s and '40s, when La Playa had cachet, big bands and orchestras playing in ballrooms, Meyer Davis, Lester Lanin, and Ellington as a matter of course and not combos jumpin' in basements. The beach adjoining would once have paraded smart-striped umbrellas and similar bathers, not battle-blasted sand.

Alone at her table, Martha found herself in serious assembly. None of the pensioners and misplaced tourists from up the stairs; here were men, a few intent couples, some nursing mere cups of coffee, many tapping manic feet like the fellows playing: Frankie, with trumpet; a saxophonist, a drummer, bass player, pianist. The place dusky, elbow to elbow, dirty round the edges, the music better than good. Martha had seen the very black drummer roaming the streets in dark, wrap-the-head glasses, a spruce suit of green velvet (velvet! in this heat!), scuffed and shabby shoes, nonchalant as hell. He was to the fore in a frenzied, boppy, bopped-out version of 'How High the Moon', the sax and trumpet blowing like crazy, the pianist – a little white man with small, plump hands that pounced obscenely as if the keys were breasts of dead game birds – scurrying, crawling obsessively under the roaring, bristling thicket of sound to burst out in triumphant solo.

There was a fair amount of cry and comment from those on stage – or rather, stamp, their designated area being that size.

They pitched and rolled through 'Jumpin' at the Woodside', and then the saxophonist, who seemed in charge, a tall, shock-headed, grey-haired American, announced a title which Martha didn't follow – something about a kiss – and slid into that marshmallow sweetness of tenor sax, tyrannical in close-up – ear to brass – down dark basements.

He took this brass and built, supported by piano, drum, and bass, but far off, climbing up from marshmallow on to the scaffolding of a syncopated tremolo, as deliberately precarious as he made it lovely. He built caves that went back into memory; rolled aside boulders where forgotten moments lay in ambush; opened rooms resonant with the crash of experience rushing pell-mell nowhere. It was bitter and sweet, and the music blew up out of caves, right through a crevice in the rock, swirled with heady, incessant beat and paused to regather, offshore, with those unsettling powers that had kept them, Martha and Louis, turning uneasily from hotel bedroom always seaward.

There were high notes to finish. Martha was exhilarated, sat contained for a minute of applause and volley, then rose and ran out, along the dirty shore where tourists were said to be menaced with all kinds of night-time danger, leapt at the ruthlessly glittering heavens, burst forward, ran on. She spread herself across different time zones: London was four hours ahead and Tokyo thirteen; Roy slept as Martha dashed, while Louis, always rushing, shuffled his music before rehearsal. Running gave Martha a weightless sense that caused each man to slip from his hour and scoot at will round the earth's surface. She skidded, nearly toppled, slowed, turned and loped back to El Palomar, dropped clothes to the floor and fell instantly unconscious.

In the morning she woke and rose with unusual zest, bathed, sat down to write and went on for days. She wrote, revised, discarded and typed at dramatic pace, aware that clouds erupted above the Atlantic, that warm air blew feverish condiments through open windows, that music blew about her head. Strange thoughts came to mind: Louis's mother had died when he was a boy at school, and all the way home he told himself it wasn't true, that she'd meet him at the station the way she always met him. Martha had remembered this when a friend of hers, an elderly man to whom she'd been close and within an hour or two of visiting – she had something to show him – had died without illness and she couldn't believe it, had for weeks after the funeral telephoned his flat, sure he would answer. Of all her belongings, it was that picture, which she'd never shown him, that most reminded her of Ralph Cassell.

Downing pen and covering portable, she sometimes went to 'hang around' with Frankie and his mates: Pharaoh the drummer; 'Basie' Burns-at-the-piano, who was likable despite his hands and a damn good player; Mel-on-bass and Hector Ming, who led and blew. Hector had roamed and rattled the world as jazz musicians sometimes do, come to work in Santa Rosa, married a local girl – one of the jelly babies barely grown, from the look of her photo – lived with his family up in the hills. The Hector Ming Quintet was often a sextet or quartet, depending on which of his friends could be lured to Santa Rosa for lengthy stints, and appeared to have its share of dogged expatriate fans and eastern seaboard enthusiasts.

Martha had wondered what jazzmen talked about among themselves. Did they, like members of orchestras known to her, give vent to rumbling stomachs, fears of unemployment, the cost of answering services – everything in fact except the joys of music? Discovery of this banality had been one of the few disillusions packed in Louis's dowry. Frankie and Pharaoh and Mel and 'Basie' Burns had a reminiscent turn of mind, and there was no such thing as an answering service around Santa Rosa.

'Honey,' Pharaoh said, 'I can sleep anywhere – standin' up, lyin' down, doesn't matter. I once spent, must have been forty, fifty days on the road an' we slept ever' night in the bus cuz in them days, the '50s, you didn't have black and white sleepin' in the same motel.'

'We had a roadie that could never sleep except in bed,' said Mel-on-bass. 'Used to survive on brandy was it, or mebbe whiskey? I forget. Anyway he was never drunk that I could see an' all night he would keep busy writin' songs. Pretty fine, they were. Still play some of them. Dead now, I guess.'

Frankie and 'Basie' were younger than the others, had more of the savour of life beyond the pale and some of its conventions. They all seemed happy to have her come and go and Martha thought – or fancied – they lived more like people in touch with their work than many folk she knew about. Their electric feet were always on the hop and their comfortably shambolic lives could turn up steel and wicked variations in quick, impromptu solo.

Hector told Martha a lot about the island, reminded her of Columbus who discovered it (he'd heard of the neighbouring bones), of Ponce de Léon the settler, of all the Francis Drakes who'd attacked in vain, the ruffian Spaniards who ripened as grandees, the African slaves brought to pan gold and to plant the sugar. All these forgotten things which people here just lived, which showed in their features, their jelly-baby children and the husbands' ears against pregnant bellies. Like if someone should question her attitude to Roy, or to Louis – 'It's just love, y'know,' she'd say – or ask what writing she was taking so long about – 'Just a book,' she'd answer, diverting her pen on to fragmentary postcards for Louis and Roy:

Have discovered old-town cobblestones, those blue ones, not cobbles *at all*, but cast in slag iron from Spanish foundries.

Or

Ming & Co play mean version of 'Sent for You Yesterday and Here You Come Today' – which is one way of saying I'll be back soon, with quite a few typed pages!

'You can't leave us without coming out to the house,' said Ming, inviting her with 'all the boys' for the whole of Sunday, a barbecue, almost certainly a little playing. With Pharaoh and Frankie, in a fairly wrecked – air-conditioned – rental, Martha went up again to those intensely cultivated mountains, passed tobacco fields, wound the car round curves full of trees entwined by clashing bougainvillaea, and climbed out at a wooden hacienda like the inn where she and Louis had spent some days. The air here was fresher than at Descansado. Ileana, who was Hector's wife, pressed cool hands into all of theirs, and introduced Chiqui, Ramón, and Edgardo, brown-eyed children under twelve. There were numerous aunts, cousins, nieces, nephews, uncles; the women sat together, very coiffed and cheerful, speaking that machine-gun Spanish into which Martha could never find recognizable entry; all the men gathered near Hector and Ileana's probable brothers as they turned pig on a spit and brushed it now and again with oil.

Martha and 'the boys' simply sat and talked.

'I'm sure I've heard of him, your husband. Louis Cinnabar. He come to New York sometimes?' asked Pharaoh, who was anchored in that city.

'Basie' Burns, an Englishman, said, 'God, how I love New York. I like to go there, sit in bars, make conversation. Trouble is I start drinkin'.'

Frankie the trumpeter said that if he ever got to London he was for certain gonna look her and 'Lewis' up.

'As we all are!' said Mel, and Martha thought how they'd almost certainly never figured her out, what she was doing there – looking 'well-tended' (as one of them put it) – living rough-and-ready in Palomar, writing like a loon, loving her husband (who was off in Tokyo), not shouting 'Freedom!' or hating men or even *saying* much of anything. But they'd never asked her a lot of questions.

When lunch had been eaten – they *stuffed* themselves on barbecued pig! – and everyone sank replete for hours, spoke in English and Spanish and sometimes merely smiled in rounds of inarticulate good will, Martha went off to walk before driving back to Descansado.

She stepped out through tropical gardens, among frangipani, along a high and fertile ridge. There was music up ahead, she thought, kept

walking on in some disbelief; it was definitely music – just a saxophone. A little further and she saw it was Hector, just blowing, up against the African-cumulus sky, the mountains lapping away behind so you almost imagined you could see the ocean. That playing was out and about but so smooth; none of its stairways, its corridors or back alleys up front or even visible, none of its furnishings wasted.

Martha, who suddenly felt like singing, did not rush forward and hug Hector but began to dance, right there on that ridge of mountain, in full view of the future and her flight to London, to Louis who was meeting her and to Roy who wasn't, with her luggage reapportioned, some of it heavier and some of it, quite a lot of it, months and miles lighter.

For Louis Jordan

David Kennedy

One midday in Memphis on the banks of the Nile
As those ancient Egyptians were strutting with style
A cat was heard to say to a dusky honeychile
In accents cute enough to make sarcophagi smile:
'The way you step a cubit has ineffable grace
So let's take a barge of burnished gold on down to my place;
And while you scan papyri or powder your face
I'll prepare a cold collation at a leisurely pace
'Cos you may look like a mummy with a dose of the flu
But I'm a rootin' Tutenkhamun and I'm rootin' for you!'
   Rootin' Tutenkhamun! (Rootin' Tutenkhamun!)
   Yeah I'm a rootin' Tutenkhamun! (He's a rootin' Tutenkhamun!)
   I hope you find me charmin' (Charmin' Tutenkhamun)
   'Cos I aim to be disarmin' (Disarmin' Tutenkhamun)
   I ain't ready for embalmin':
   'Cos I'm a rootin' Tutenkhamun and I'm rootin' for you!

By the sacred name of Horus
Professor play that chorus!

For Louis Jordan

They hopped into a chariot and drove to the Sphinx
Stopped off at an oasis where they bought a few drinks;
He whispered some suggestions as they watched the sun sink
But she rebuffed him with vehemence when he tipped her the wink:
She said: 'It's as plain as if writ hieroglyphically
Just where you stand when I say my name is Nefertiti!'
   My name is Nefertiti! (Never Nefertiti?)
   You're outa your class completely (Chichi Nefertiti)
   I certainly ain't your sweetie (Sweetie Nefertiti)
   You don't even know how to greet me (Hi there Nefertiti)
   No you could never please me:
   'Cos my name is Nefertiti and I *never* you see!

We've swung this swingin' hymnal
So let's take it home to Simbel!

A Ticket to Spare

Zinovy Zinik

Born in Moscow in 1945, Zinovy Zinik emigrated from the USSR in 1975 and since 1979 has lived in London. Two of his novels have been translated into French and an English adaptation of his recent novel, Russian Service, *was broadcast by the BBC in 1984.*

The Kiev militiaman stood and gawped. The sight of these blacks jiving away shamelessly, these blacks who had gone and sold out to bourgeois decadence and imperialism, filled him with horror. His face beaded with sweat, he was in despair: on the one hand it was just the sort of incident for calling in the riot squad; on the other, racism was on the rampage over there and, as the political instructor had told them at the briefing, jazz was 'a freedom-loving form of expression'. An expression of total incomprehension was written not just on the faces in the militia cordon; I could not believe my eyes, either. Who would have thought we would hear those sounds, see those bodies move for real, in broad daylight, in Kiev Stadium? Up there on stage, in the flesh, copying his own famous sound, was Duke himself. For goodness knows how many years his music had cut through the jamming of the various foreign 'voices', and here he was, a black with a face bleached by years of using good soap, his hair straightened, stalking in front of his buddies who were swinging away on the stage no more than ten metres from where I was sitting. A fat woman, the wife of one of the city bosses by the look of her, leant close to her husband in his sunflower-patterned shirt and whispered in a broad Ukrainian accent: 'I can't see, is he black or isn't he? And his hair's curly brown, or ginger is it?'

Her husband's sunflowers heaved as he sighed: 'Don't trouble your head, love. Just listen, eh? Listen!' And his double chin jiggled in time to 'Caravan'. The floor was throbbing with the music, and through it my feet could sense that the gigantic bust of the Leader in the entrance hall down below was also jiggling to the mighty rhythms. I had the feeling that dragging myself all the way from Moscow down here to Kiev was not going to be a complete waste of time.

'Ladies and gentlemen, I love you' – Duke spoke the classic words with which he began all his concerts; but it was one thing to know them from hearsay and quite another to see them formed by his own lips. Yes, he loved us, only he didn't say what for; like Bernard Shaw loved Russia, according to one of my well-read friends, though for all that Shaw did say: 'The Russians showed God the door, but he came bouncing back in through the window in the shape of the NKVD.' The great Duke Ellington loved the ladies and gentlemen in his Kiev audience as if he hadn't noticed the militiamen and men in plain clothes in a ring around the stadium. As I had squeezed with my ticket through the security cordon, I had seen two cops grab a kid who had tried to slip past by the elbows and hustle him away to a car. They weren't beating him up, not as far as you could see, but he was letting out this horrible squeal – from having his fingers twisted discreetly. So, everyone who made it into the concert gripped his ticket in his hot, sweaty fist as if it was a pass to another world, a visa to freedom. For me the irony was that I'd been given my ticket by a friend who'd just been refused a visa to his freedom – Jerusalem, and who had now taken to wearing a black beret and observing the Sabbath. There was a time when both of us had been greedy for the forbidden fruit of jazz, and we had equated the freedom of the music-making with freedom of speech. By the time Duke came to Kiev for the concert, though, my friend had arrived at a different concept of freedom. 'For blacks jazz is the lost Motherland. For me Judaism is the jazz the Jews have found,' he told me. And when someone in Kiev sent him a ticket for this performance of the blacks' lost Motherland, he preferred to stay in Moscow and join a hunger strike in support of the jazz the Jews had found. I didn't argue, I accepted the ticket which no ordinary Muscovite had any hope of obtaining. And I gave thanks in my heart to Judaism, or at least to the hunger strike in its support.

The great Duke, whom we had idolized from a distance as a prayer, a hymn and a classic, seemed in the flesh like a cheap jester at first. What did he think he was doing? Clowning around in drainpipe trousers, zero minus, a posturing poseur. But his over-familiarity was that of the well-practised clown, being pally with the audience was part of the job; all that free improvisation, all that jazz without those hateful music stands was an act. This much was clear: if the trombonist, say, were to fluff a single note, a drumstick would come whacking down on his head and the bassist would slice him in half with his bow. And if my friend was right about a Motherland lost and jazz gained, then religion and destiny also turned out to be a well-rehearsed circus routine: to the man in the audience truth seems like a circus trick performed by somebody in a black top hat; the clown, though, knows that any trick depends on rules, on discipline, on sleight of hand and that there can be no question of cheating. Rationalizing *post factum*, the tricks were being performed on me, though at the time I believed I was a spectator, and as I watched Duke prancing I envied myself and sympathized hypocritically with starving Judaism; in this arena, wholly inappropriate for circus stunts, stuffed as it was with militiamen and the overheated wives of Party functionaries, with the plaster bust of the macabre fantast shaking in the entrance, the great bandleader performed acrobatic miracles. The tighter the musicians he held in his power wound our nerves up with the music, the more this ringmaster acted as though nothing special was happening. He created a spectacle out of nothing, producing sounds the way a conjuror pulls a flood of streamers out of an empty top hat. He wandered absent-mindedly across the stage and then, as if he had suddenly remembered an old joke, he fetched a rattle from one corner, wound it pensively, like a clockwork toy, so it made an ironic 'trr-rr-rr-i-k-k-k' in the pause that instantly intruded. Or he paced in circles twisting an ordinary jam jar filled with pebbles, and these pebbles made a shooshing noise like shingle in the waves, free and easy among the rumble of artillery fire. Then, while the bass and drums were working themselves and their audience into a frenzy, flailing wildly in a cage of four notes, he squatted down on his haunches and began tapping away at a pair of bongos, as a man waiting for service in a restaurant taps on the table.

Then the music changed: Duke's famous trumpet-solo player picked up his golden horn and pressed his lips to the mouthpiece. All of a sudden his cheeks ballooned out as far as his ears and on these zeppelins he soared, the wrinkles on his forehead giving him a slightly offended look.

The trumpet stuck out like a giant cigarette and its full, generous sound was like a welcoming wave of the hand, high above and far away: yes, of course, everything will be fine if you pretend everything *is* fine and allow yourself the occasional grumble and the odd tear, even. For half an hour these heartfelt appeals built, then suddenly he stumbled on something he seemed never to have encountered before, and it wasn't at all clear how he was going to get himself out of this tangled dialogue with himself, a dialogue he had driven himself into by his own witty calls. Forced as he now was to come up with responses that were no less slick, he puffed out his cheeks and matched every chuckle in the top register with melancholy irony in the bottom one. He faltered, then stopped altogether. Without raising his eyes, as though ashamed of having given in, he took the trumpet from his lips, wiped the sweat from his face and growled into the microphone: 'Only cats dig me is Jews. Slavery in Egypt!' He waited a second before rounding off this carefully rehearsed flop with a final blare on his trumpet. The stadium erupted; whistles from the veteran jazz buffs and applause from the novices who didn't know you're supposed to stomp your feet when the jazz gets to you, not clap your hands. But neither the veterans nor the novices had really followed what, in actual fact, the trumpeter had growled into the microphone; but I had heard this remark, which slipped out so easily back in the Bible belt, on records and I relished the thought of how I would go back to Moscow and, oh so cool, tell how this American black had made a complaint that would have rocked the Kiev audience if they had only understood it.

Later, when my Kiev phantasmagoria was over, I remembered this remark in the stillness of the hushed stadium as the first, if veiled, hint of the events which would soon develop at breakneck speed. But at that time, during the concert, I noticed only that while the applause thundered on a plain-clothes man standing in the gangway bent towards a cop and whispered something in his ear. The cop frowned and went scarlet. Surprisingly, though, it was an initiative from below, from the over-excited masses, which put paid to these provocative forms of expression. During the interval an usherette came out into the gangway with a stack of programmes for sale. This was a fatal mistake and even putting the cop to stand next to her was no help: there was a rush for the programme with the souvenir photo, everybody was desperate to lay hands on tangible proof of having been in that other world of hitherto unknown freedom. First the crowd from the lower rows of seats made a rush at the usherette for these precious programmes. Those who couldn't push through began to go round the back via the next gangway, through the foyer, out and then back down the steps from above; sunflower bald spots tangled with sunflowers on bosoms. I watched in despair as my hopes of hearing out this music smashed into splinters along with the rows of seating. These people had taken freedom literally: they felt everybody had the right to participate in the conjuring trick and that the golden trumpet on the front of the programme should be common property, seeing as its music called for universal love. I was one of the first to realize the game was up

and it was time to leg it before they decided to break mine for me –
you could hear the scrunch of benches and skulls from the gangway
and the police cars wailing out in the square in front of the stadium.
In jazz I prefer the pauses.

After all that racket, the normal rumble of the city seemed just like
one of those wonderful pauses. But not for long. I stood in the square
a moment, all wound up, wild, then turned blindly down a side
street. Feeling that it was I, myself who had gone and got me thrown
out on my neck, I tried not to look in people's faces. Because I had
gone to the concert straight from the train, I felt as though I were still
in a station and I kept imagining those penetrating smells of garlic
sausage and hard-boiled eggs that always go with station life. The
passers-by looked to me like the crowds of country folk at Moscow
stations, armed with string bags and out to raid the food shops.
'Hayseeds,' I thought, glancing at them furtively hurrying God knew
where, until I suddenly remembered I wasn't in Moscow. This was
Kiev and I couldn't expect to see the familiar old faces. It wasn't a
station crowd I was surrounded by, just ugly mugs, ones which had
haunted Gogol, who hailed from these parts. True, for him the whole
of Russia was something out of a nightmare, was one big ugly mug;
but then I'm not Gogol and I just wanted to be back in Moscow, away
from the faces of this city, the city of Gogol's evil, subterranean
goblin, Viy. What I meant by a familiar face is hard to say. Anybody
whose eyes signalled 'one of us', I suppose.

I studied the neighbourhood with annoyance, trying to detect in
the buildings some reflection of the warmth I failed to find in
people's faces. The shop signs, all in Ukrainian, irritated the eye
with their stupid incomprehensible familiarity – the similarity
between Russian and Ukrainian, that is like that between man and
ape, a similarity which serves only to emphasize the differences
between them and which will prevent any kind of merger, because
each of them will always insist that the other comes lower on the
Darwinian scale.

Every so often the one face I did know in this city swam into view
on a poster stuck up on a wall of one of the buildings, which in the
luxurious autumn sunlight resembled stale, or maybe overdone,
cakes: the face of the great Duke Ellington. It was a three-tier poster
in Russian, Ukrainian and English, urging people with triple
insistence to go to an event that was over already and merely teased
the memory with that heavenly sound, all the more unreal now for
having been drowned out by the cracking of bones and the screech of
police whistles. I dropped into a post office and tried to scribble a
card to Moscow using the words that had flashed across my mind
during the performance. I gave up in the end and tore the picture

postcard into tiny pieces.

I had to hang around for a train till the following morning, but had absolutely no inclination to go back to my hotel, more of a hostel or a communal squat, really. It would have been rather like the philosopher Khoma Brut in that Gogol story going back to the chapel to confront Viy at the coffin of the old witch. The hotel was the sort of place where the Soviet travelling factory rep, stripped to his vest and braces, stuffing himself with pilchards to go with his favourite fruit-and-berry wine, stares at you with sleepy eyes and belches: 'Shut the window would you, Comrade. Draughty.' Unnerved by the free for all at the stadium, I had fled of my own free will from the second half of the freedom I was always going on about. And I could hear the voice of the Pioneer that had been lurking in my soul since childhood ask the embarrassing question: 'How are you going to be able to look your comrades in the eye?' This trip wasn't going to end up as material for a hilariously funny story for me to peddle in Moscow, a story I'd begun working on while still on the train to Kiev. But what was I supposed to do in this city till morning? By this time I had wandered down the steep hill to the old low-lying suburb of Podol, the Dnieper gleaming in the still weather, and lost myself in the maze of narrow streets. I was limping now, my heel rubbed raw. It felt as if every step I took rocked this enchanted city: ripe conkers hurtled down through the golden foliage overhead and landed on the asphalt with a noise like cracking knuckles, bouncing up and away to one side as if aimed at my back.

My throat was parched from all the walking (your larynx dries up from walking in much the same way words do when you are separated from somebody for a long time) and I turned down the steps of a basement bar I happened on. It was cool down there, empty and shadowy, and the air held the acid tang of wine from the barrel. I downed a tumbler of dry sherry in one at the zinc-topped counter, wiped my lips and was on my way to the door when I saw somebody beckoning to me out of the semi-darkness of one corner. 'Oi, balabosse. C'mover'ere, boss!' What were they calling me for? It was crazy, but it was obviously me they wanted because there was nobody else in the place, except the barmaid, and she'd vanished behind a curtain. In the corner two Kievites, bottle in hand, were sizing me up. Both looked completely out of place in best black suits and ties, in white sweat-stained shirts, frayed at the collar. By the look of them they'd either been to a funeral, a wedding or a Party meeting, all of which amount to much the same in the end.

'They look flash enough, but they don't half pinch!' One of them was pulling a face as he inspected his gleaming new shoes. He muttered something about having to be off home to the missus and it was obvious that this wasn't the first time he had said it. His comrade, who had meanwhile splashed a generous measure of sherry into my tumbler, retorted that it was in the nature of things for a new boot to pinch, and if your foot felt comfortable it, the boot, wouldn't be new any more, would it, and the same, as it happened, went for a woman. Now his old grandad had made him a present of his pocket watch, but he hadn't heard a tick out of it for days. His grandad had given him this gold watch to remember him by, so his grandad's memory wasn't ticking right, not that he was complaining. He held the gold watch to his comrade's ear: 'Can you hear it? What did I tell you? And you go on about boots!' Evidently they wanted me to arbitrate between new shoes and grandad's watch. We clinked glasses.

'You from Moscow? Another stinking Muscovite? Have a drink!' said the separatist with the gold watch. 'We're not long back from Moscow ourselves. Big place, Moscow. But you'll never find sherry like this there, eh?' He frowned at his glass.

His comrade with the new shoes backed him up: ' 'S a fact. No sherry.' He shook his head. 'I was reading in a book by one of them banned Rooshian writers, no sherry in their station buffets. There's cows' udders they say, but sherry's off. Stuff cows' udders, I say!'

The separatist with his grandfather's watch fuelled the flames by pouring more sherry: 'What was it one of them bloody Rooshian poets said, that one they were always ramming down your throat at school – Pooshkin: "What udder name means aught to you"! So, you stinking Muscovite, wha's your name?' Every gesture could have finished either with them cracking me over the head with a glass or inviting me to drink up. They weren't so much unsophisticated as plain drunk.

'Zinovy.' I gave my name with some trepidation.

'Wha', wha'?' the owner of the watch demanded with a hiccough. 'Nor they can't mend a watch properly in Moscow.' He had changed tack. 'I went to get my watch fixed in that village of yours. It doesn't tick any more, I said. And the watchmaker, y'know, did he ever have a conk and a half, what was it you said your name was?'

I repeated it.

'Well then,' he put himself back on course, 'there he was sitting there, the ugliest-looking watchmaker you ever set eyes on!' He shook his head.

'Moscow!' began the one with the tight shoes. 'I ask this bloke behind the counter: will they be too tight or not? You should've seen his hooter. What did you say you were called?' He turned to me.

'Zinovy,' I repeated.

'An ugly-looking bugger, but what do you expect?' he concluded with a sigh.

They could not stop harping on about the size of the watchmaker's and the shoe saleman's noses, and when they asked me my name a fourth time, I followed the promptings of cowardice and blurted: 'It's a Polish name, by the way.'

They both hooted with derision and even seemed to sober up a bit: 'Polish? Zinovy! Oh yes, very Polish! You've a lot to thank your parents for, giving you that very Polish name,' and they shook their heads and guffawed. 'Polish, he says, Polish!'

But I kept my head and asked slyly, weren't they proud of their national hero Bogdan Khmelnitsky? And didn't they know that Khmelnitsky had another name besides Bogdan – Zinovy Bogdan Khmelnitsky. 'Check in the Soviet calendar.' I downed what remained of the sherry in my glass in triumph. I said I had been born on the same day as the great Ukrainian patriot, the architect of the Ukraine's reunification with Russia, and my parents, both strong internationalists, had called me Zinovy in honour of Khmelnitsky.

Perhaps the two Kievites really weren't too sure about these details, because they both sat staring at me with their mouths open. But it was more likely that I hadn't thought through exactly what sort of an independent Ukraine they stood for, and whether it was the sort Bogdan Khmelnitsky had sold out to Russian autocracy. Because they gulped in surprise and then bore down on me together: 'Don't think we don't know what you are. It's as plain as the nose on your face. Yeh, but you and your kind make out all of us look the same, seen one you seen us all. So you get back to them. Go on, git!' They both stood and advanced on me.

'Where to?' I was on my way to the door.

'Over the road. You blind as well as thick? Get over that road.'

I shot outside and scurried along the pavement, keeping a sharp lookout over my shoulder. The two separatists stood outside the bar waving their fists, either threatening me or showing me which way to go. I crossed the street, followed a high stone wall, turned a corner and into a dead end. I stopped, not knowing what to do next. The cul-de-sac was deserted, overhung with golden, dust-powdered branches, and seemingly uninhabited. Not one window looked down on you in this useless appendix of the city, a blind gut. The heel of my shoe held my chafed foot in an iron grip; I had no desire to go back out into the street and perhaps have to face the two black-suited separatists. In a lather of panic, as always when compelled to knock at some unfamiliar door, I walked up to a pair of iron gates layered with dusty paint, in an attempt to find a yard or some other way out of the dead end. A breeze stirred and once again I felt myself under fire from the chestnuts that came thudding down on to the asphalt. I leant my head against the metal of the gates, as if shielding myself against this vicious yet impotent hail, and as I waited for an end to the plocking and the scritching of the conkers, which came flying out of their splitting shells as they fell, I unconsciously pressed my hand into some embossed metal ornamentation. Suddenly I felt myself falling forwards; part of the gates, the part I'd been leaning on, turned out to be a little door and had swung open. Barely managing to keep my feet, I stumbled into a yard and almost fell on my knees in front of a man who was sitting on a bench right beside the gates. The iron door slammed shut on its powerful spring.

The man, dressed in an unseasonable black raincoat, did not get up. He raised his black hat, adjusted his glasses and asked: 'Where you from?'

'I'm lost,' I said.

'You're not from Kiev? Then what for you are in Kiev?' He shrugged, irritated. 'Maybe you should have your eyes tested? Don't you see the posters on every corner? Up in black and white, in three languages: Russian, Ukrainian,' he folded down his fingers, 'and in German. Perhaps the young man can't read?'

'It's English on the poster, not German. Russian, Ukrainian and a bit in English.' I corrected him mechanically, looking round the courtyard, which had a forbidding padlocked building at the far end.

'English?' The man in the hat grinned. 'Does it really matter? Today in German, tomorrow in English: report to the crossroads by the cemetery, have your identity papers with you, your money, valuables, also warm clothing, otherwise you are liable to be shot. Or perhaps the young man is a goy?' He lifted his spectacles, the better to study me. 'How did you get here on this day of sorrow?'

'By accident,' I mumbled.

'Nobody gets here by accident,' he said as he watched the evening breeze scatter the conker shells.

I tried to think of an excuse to get away. 'I'm looking for a chemist's. Is there one near here?' I asked, suddenly mindful of my chafed heel. 'My foot's sore. I need a plaster,' I continued, for added conviction.

'There is a chemist. Round the corner to the right is an excellent chemist's.' Once again he shrugged his shoulders. 'But what for you need a plaster? A plaster will be no help in the next world.'

I made a clumsy bow and tried to retreat backwards to the iron door. After it had clanged shut behind me with a screech of its spring, my eyes resolved its metal ornamentation into a Star of David: the yard, then, belonged to the local synagogue. But the neighbourhood madman noticed neither my bow, nor the slamming of the metal door; he was absorbed in contemplation of a conker shell which had landed at his feet.

The day which had begun with such a swing, with driving rhythms and blaring trumpets, was ending in nightmare. I bit my lip as I walked, either because I felt I had been somehow insulted or because of the pain I was in. I tried not to put any weight on my sore heel, tried not to glance at the bar on my left, turned right then right again at the first corner, as the madman had told me. The street dropped away in front of me, down towards the Dnieper. It was lined with houses, chipped and pockmarked like battered old suitcases. Their shadows lengthened in the evening sun, as though these were giant suitcases being carried downhill by unseen travellers, a living queue jostling towards nobody knew what. And I hurried on down after them.

On the first corner a man in a white chemist's overall stood under a shop sign, CHEMIST, as if expecting me. He was smoking a cigarette, staring into the distance after the shadows as they crept down the slope. He was watching the sunset and smoking, something that these days happens only in southern towns where people have not forgotten how to say farewell at evening to the day. I waited some distance away on the edge of the pavement, trying to decide whether to interrupt his contemplation of the setting sun, spinning in a dusty, golden haze at the bottom of the street. He finished his cigarette, ground it out against his heel and threw the butt down a grating. He turned to me and asked abruptly: 'Can I help?' The huge length of his shadow was scarcely an exaggeration for he was, indeed, immensely tall. I hardly came up to his shoulder. He looked me up and down, and he didn't peer short-sightedly and blink the way you'd expect a chemist to. This look was a blast from both barrels of a shotgun.

'I need a plaster. I'm lost. I've rubbed my heel raw,' I said helplessly.

'Don't you know what the time is? I'm closed. Who sent you to me?'

I hadn't realized Kiev chemists required a letter of introduction. I glanced at my watch. It showed a ridiculously early hour, and putting it to my ear I found it had stopped. Watch on the blink, shoes killing me, the two separatists, one with a bust watch and the other with shoes that pinched, their troubles coincided with mine – this city was bewitched, damn it – all this was like a clenched fist shoving me in the back: 'Get back to where you belong!' I plucked up courage: 'They sent me here from the synagogue.'

'The synagogue?' He hesitated. 'Very well. You can have a plaster,' and he began to unlock the shop door.

While he jangled his bunch of keys, I babbled some sort of self-justification, the way everybody in the Soviet Union does to shop assistants. 'I was at the jazz concert today, utter shambles, the whole thing fell apart, barely managed to get out in one piece, then I went and rubbed my heel wandering around Kiev.'

When he heard the word 'jazz', the chemist turned and looked at me hard again. His eyes combed the street, then suddenly he bent and asked, in a whisper this time: 'You from Moscow?'

I nodded, mesmerized by this performance. He said no more, threw open the shop door and pushed me inside. His supercilious aloofness had vanished. He snapped the lock shut and hurried behind the counter, where he began rummaging among packages and boxes. He found something, looked at me again, and repeated his previous question: 'From Moscow? A plaster?'

I smiled guiltily, as if by chafing my heel I had committed an unpardonable error, a mortal sin. I tried to meet his searching gaze, then took to studying my own reflection in the glass-fronted cupboards full of phials, jars and, on one shelf, a mountain of spectacles, or rather of empty frames without lenses, as if they had been stripped from the dead for salvage.

'Here we are. Your plaster.' He placed a circle of elasticized sticking plaster on the counter. 'Nothing else? You're sure?'

After a day like this one I wasn't sure about anything. My head was throbbing after the sherry, my mouth tasted as though somebody had given me a good punch in the teeth. I remembered I'd forgotten to bring toothpaste with me. 'You wouldn't have any toothpaste?' I asked hesitantly.

His lips parted in an unexpectedly cordial smile. For some reason my request made him terribly happy. 'Toothpaste? Of course! Why didn't you ask before?' He rummaged behind the counter again. 'Which kind of toothpaste? Which sort do you prefer?'

His enthusiasm struck me as rather absurd and I said I really wasn't bothered which kind. Everything about this chemist's struck me as absurd. Actually, this was the very first time I had ever been inside a shop after hours, i.e. face to face, alone with an assistant in an empty shop. In the back of my head I could feel the door locked shut behind me. 'I'm really not bothered,' I said again, my thoughts returning to toothpaste.

'What do you mean, not bothered?' the chemist fussed. 'You've come all the way from Moscow. You are from Moscow, aren't you?'

I nodded. 'Oh, all right then. Peppermint will be fine.'

This conversation was beginning to sound like something out of a spy story. It was obvious he was interested in a lot more than he dared say. 'I don't have change, you realize. I've cashed up already,' the chemist said before I had produced even a kopeck out of my pocket. It struck me he might be trying to squeeze some extra money out of me, a desperate passing customer. All I wanted to do was sit down, anywhere, then and there, or best of all lie down – even that hotel would have done – lie down with the blanket pulled up over my head and shut out this city. I certainly didn't want to start arguing, so I put my hand in my pocket and, ignoring all the change I had which would have been enough for a dozen plasters, produced a rouble note.

The chemist grabbed it and began waving it about. 'For you, though, I will try and find change. Let's go.' He took my elbow and guided me to the back door. His grip on my arm was firm: resistance would have been useless. On the other side of the door a narrow staircase led downwards and a dim light burned at the foot. I was marched down.

I tried to protest: 'What are you doing to me?'

The chemist only whispered: 'Ssshh! Just one more step now!'

Filtering out through a crack of light I heard a plangent sound, either of weeping or singing, as unsettling as the prospect of the denouement to come. A door was thrown open. After the gloom of the staircase, the light in this room was dazzling. Twelve men were seated around a long table. They all seemed very much alike, the way a row of Party functionaries sitting arms folded on the platform can do sometimes. As my eyes gradually grew accustomed to the light, I was able to decode the points of similarity between the members of this conclave: every single one of them was wearing a black beret. Each had a dog-eared volume lying open in front of him. The table, spread with a white cloth, was dominated by two objects – an uncorked bottle of deep-red wine and a seven-branched candlestick. Now I knew where I was. I was among the Jews.

'The man from Moscow.' The chemist pushed me forward. I stood there blinking in the light. All twelve berets swivelled slowly towards me. The last to do so belonged to the man sitting at the head of the table with his back to me. I expected to see a grey beard and bushy eyebrows. But the face that stared at me was hard and youthful, younger than any of the others there, one of those bold, reckless faces I had seen in the company of my Moscow friend. He looked at me in absolute silence, then turned to the chemist and said in a light dry tenor: 'Not him.' And the twelve all went back to their books again and once more took up their mumbling – was it wailing or chanting? As far as they were concerned I no longer existed. But I knew I was among my own; that they were gathered here in secret; that they were expecting somebody, an emissary from Moscow; that I wasn't him. I wasn't the emissary. But I did know what was going on.

B Flat, Bebop, Scat

Perhaps I had made my exodus from the second half of the blacks' lost Motherland only to finish up in the jazz the Jews had found. I could tell them about all the people who might be their emissary, I could come up with the phrase I had picked up from my friend, 'aleikum salaam'. I was well up in these things: Zion, the sabbath and keep off the salami. But I didn't say salaam to the leader of the Jews for confiding in me, a Prodigal Son. Because I'd lost my nerve again and had a suspicion that after the fatal words 'Not him', the interpretation the chemist and the others of the twelve would put on every step I had taken on the way to that brightly lit room was that I was a grass and a double-dealer. And anything I might say about me, too, belonging to the chosen people would only go to prove it. The chemist began shoving me towards the door. At the top of the stairs, before he finally sent me packing, he dug a heap of coins out of his pocket and forced them into my hand: 'Your change! Your change!'

I was standing in the dark in a strange city, the conkers thudding down, with a defunct watch and a very sore heel, with a filthy taste in my mouth which didn't go until I reached Moscow, where I was drily informed that I had been in Kiev on the anniversary of the slaughter of the Jews, on the day prayers were held in secret for the victims of Babi Yar. But I, I, a person who has always been received by everybody, everywhere, on every occasion, had had the door of the one place in the world I most wanted to be in at that particular moment slammed shut without ceremony in my face, and there was just one thing I wanted to find out: who was it those men were expecting in that Kiev basement? And I don't just mean my friend, who might have found himself in my place had he not given me that ticket which happened to be spare.

Translated from Russian by Frank Williams

Double Bass

Sue May

There is a tree in the orchestra.
It talks softly, like a bear.
It stands holding its hat by the rim.
Bashful.
It has quiet conversations
with drums and paint brushes.
It is a humble instrument.
The people who play it are shy and serious.
They close their eyes to hear.
Sometimes playing is excruciating;
their fingers run up and down like spiders.
Sometimes everything is gentle.
They close their eyes to hear,
touch the strings gingerly.
The wood talks,
it murmurs like a person in their sleep
when you wonder what they mean.
It can't be fierce but it can keep a secret.
It looks solid
but it sounds sad sometimes
and stands on one leg.

A Bit of a Scrape

Campbell Burnap

Campbell Burnap was born in 1939, to Scottish parents in Derby. At nineteen, he emigrated to Wellington, New Zealand, where he was a civil servant during the day and a fledgling trombonist at night. After six years in Australia, he returned to England in 1969, where he has managed to work as a professional jazz musician ever since. A qualified junior-school teacher, he occasionally appears as an extra in films and on television. He is currently with Acker Bilk's band.

On the day of the school dance it had seemed to Charlie that the lunch bell would never ring. But at last, there it was, lurching about in the belfry, while feet below, a small, duty-rostered boy furiously yanked the trailing end of its stout rope. A moment before, the assembly hall had been deserted and as silent as a forest, its only inhabitants the austere marble busts of Victorian founders and philanthropists who, down the years, had stared stiffly across at each other from their pedestals. Now, with the explosion from the tower, classroom doors burst open, releasing scores of blazered young barbarians.

This yelping army headed at speed for the refectory and Charlie nearly crashed into his friend Chris as they raced to get a good place in the queue. When they got there they could see the other two in excited conversation a few yards ahead. Shouts and waves were exchanged: nothing in particular – just a flurry of gestures that transmitted a delicious anxiety about the evening ahead, about their musical debut.

With Christmas rolling up and exams already out of the way, staff and pupils were in relaxed mood. Four hundred senior students looked forward to their annual dance. Word had got round, too, that the Chris Bland Quartet would be giving its first ever public performance at the dance, and so for Chris and Charlie, and Mick and Dave, lunch that day was a rowdy affair: a few close pals making a beeline for their table, either to josh them a little or to wish them luck.

Chris had ordered a final rehearsal to be held in the gymnasium immediately after lunch – 'just to give it a last-minute polish'.

Meanwhile, Charlie bit happily into his Christmas pudding. He was feeling like quite a big-shot.

Chris Bland was over six feet tall and wore size twelve shoes. He was the youngest of his family and, although almost sixteen, was still the shortest person at home. There was very little in it, however, with his mother just hanging on to an advantage of perhaps an inch or so. She was a music teacher, and so Chris had benefited from an early introduction to crotchets and quavers. Taking up the clarinet, he had made quick progress – but at the age of fourteen shocked his parents and amused his friends by ditching the school orchestra and joining a semi-professional dance band. From then on, his regular Saturday-night gig at the Miner's Welfare Club would pocket him more than twice as much as his friends could earn from a whole week of trudging around the suburbs with morning newspapers.

This had caused no resentment; on the contrary, it worked in his favour, and he was even more admired about a year later when he managed to persuade the stuffy Head of Music, Miss Mycroft, to allow him to hold weekly jazz-record recitals – using the precious school gramophone. Gradually, jazz became the consuming passion of this amiable and gangling character: he soon had the music room packed to the doors at his record sessions – even if some who attended were there only for the novelty value.

Charlie had been among the first converts. He listened closely to the 78-rpm records Chris hauled along each week, and just as closely to his keen summary at the end of each tune.

'Now that was Bunk Johnson on trumpet,' Chris said one day as he slipped the completed disc back into its heavy cardboard cover. 'He'd disappeared for years, you know, but then someone found him working out in the Louisiana ricefields. Well, they bought him a new set of false teeth and managed to get him blowin' again; soon after that, he was making all these wonderful sounds . . . very distinctive tone, Bunk . . . actually, his full name was William Geary "Bunk"

Johnson – born New Orleans, December 27th 1879, died New Iberia, July 7th 1949.'

Charlie and a few others listened respectfully; the dates had been recited from memory, and in tones of reverence – a little melancholy sigh squeezing through Chris's lips as he reached across for the next record. Unfortunately, *some* who crushed into those earlier record sessions were less dedicated than others, and the mention of false teeth had sent a small group of girls off into helpless giggling at the back of the room. Chris heard them and fixed an icy eye in their direction. This only made them worse, and tears of laughter and suppressed hilarity started to trickle down their cheeks. One of the girls started to mime the face of a toothless hag.

'ANYONE WHO THINKS JAZZ IS A JOKE CAN PISS OFF NOW!' thundered Chris.

This stunned everyone, especially the offending bunch who, in a moment, gathered up their satchels and marched stonily out of the room – led by a large girl whose father was a vicar. They were not seen again.

The weeding-out process continued: another two girls asked – quite pleasantly, it seemed to Charlie – what Chris thought of 'all these latest records that keep being played on the wireless'.

'Whose records?' asked Chris suspiciously.

'Well . . . Elvis Presley and Bill Haley,' they chirped back, at the same time throwing a dreamy little look in each other's direction – obviously sharing a fantasy about the singers.

Chris paused before offering his critical analysis: 'They're both *crap!*'

'*They are not!*' squealed the two girls in unison. The gooey expressions had been blasted right off their faces.

'I'm sorry, but they *are*,' said Chris firmly. 'I've seen both of them on television . . . and I'm sorry, it's all . . . well, it's all *rubbish*! It's all visual, that crap . . . I mean . . . there's nothing *underneath*, no real *feeling* . . . it's not from the heart. People like them are driving around in Cadillacs, and all *that*! How can you be sincere if you're driving around in a bloody *Cadillac*? You can't. It's all bloody show-biz and marketing – that's all *that* is. They're conning you . . . you're the mugs, but you don't realize it.'

The two girls refused to hear another word and were getting up; but Chris hadn't finished.

'If you want to hear singing from the heart, then you have to go to the men who've known deprivation . . . Furry Lewis . . . Blind Lemon Jefferson . . . people like *that*!'

'Ooohhh . . . Blind Lemon *Meringue* to *you*!' shouted one of the girls bitterly – and she turned to her friend – 'We both know why *he* hates Elvis, don't we Enid; it's because he's *jealous!*' The door slammed mightily.

Charlie observed that there was, after all, a less amiable side to Chris. He also noticed that the jazz-appreciation group was running very short of girls – a social defect which naturally led to a few boys drifting away. But gradually things settled into a more regular routine, with the weekly sessions supported by a small, but dependable, bunch of enthusiasts. Sometimes a teacher would drop in to listen for ten minutes or so, and this bestowed a valued stamp of approval upon the group. Miss Mycroft never came.

Whether or not Charlie had been consciously looking for 'a cause', there was no doubt that he had found one in the revival of traditional jazz. Of all the school crowd it was *he* who became really close with Chris. Soon they were both introduced to an older circle of collectors in the town and were made very welcome; nobody minded their school blazers or their naïveté. It was flattering to be invited to offer opinions and to share beer at these more mature recitals – fortnightly affairs, held in little terraced houses, always following a set pattern.

First, everyone would congregate in the kitchen to find a glass, pool drinks and swop gossip. After a while they would move through to the lounge to claim a seat or a cushion. The business of selecting the records and operating the gramophone was a chore both jealously claimed and lovingly performed by that particular evening's host. As soon as the needle dropped into the groove the listeners would stare at the Axminster's fading flowers, occasionally letting out little grunts of satisfaction or nodding their heads knowingly at a well-loved phrase. At the end of each 'playing' there was a ripple of appreciation and some heads shook slowly in pleasurable disbelief.

Then, after a few seconds given up to reflection, someone might speak. 'Very nice, that. But you know, I don't think Louis ever quite reached the same heights on this thirties stuff as he did ten years before with the Hot Fives.'

'Yer *joking*,' interrupted a huge handle-bar moustache from somewhere beyond a confusion of smoke and pipe. Lower down, where the visibility was better, Charlie and Chris could make out a pair of brown sandals, some baggy cord trousers and the beginnings of an Arctic-gauge pullover. A large fist clung on to a pewter tankard.

The moustache continued: ' 'Aven't you 'eard things wi' t'big band in 1935 when 'e does "Thanks a Million" and "Swing That Music"?'

'Er . . . no. Can't say I have.'

'Ooohhh . . . *well then!*' whooped the moustache, 'then you shall 'ear 'em my friend . . . then you shall 'ear 'em!'

The curly pipe was dumped firmly in the ashtray and at once the haze lifted, revealing the bushy eyebrows and moist forehead of their host. He drained the tankard impressively, flopped forward on to his knees – still murmuring 'then you shall 'ear 'em' – and crawled away behind the sofa towards a cupboard which housed Louis Armstrong, 1935.

The first speaker worked as a clerk at the Gas Board during the day, and his two passions in life were tending his small allotment and, to a lesser extent, jazz. He had always been unwilling to admit that he might know more about marrows and cucumbers than about banjos and trombones. Now he was wishing he had kept his mouth firmly shut. Everyone else looked smugly across their drinks at the unfortunate wretch who'd displayed such surprising ignorance.

The two novices loved evenings like these and learned a great deal from them. Soon they could talk – with more and more confidence – about the range of styles in jazz; about the influence of early ragtime; how black music could often be distinguished, stylistically, from white; about old blues singers. They discovered specialist magazines and were astonished to see that people all over the world shared their passion – including the King of Thailand! Radio programmes promising even the slightest whiff of jazz flavour were tracked down and 'circled' in the *Radio Times*.

Best of all, though, were the Sunday-night band concerts held at the local Playhouse Theatre. The boys always got into town early and took up a position in a darkened shop entrance across from the stage door. From here they could keep an eye out for the arrival of the coach bringing the musicians up from London. They watched them straggle out on to the pavement. Some were stretching, some swearing and they gazed about dolefully. Others had whisky bottles in their hands. Their accents were unfamiliar and varied. From across in the shadows, Chris and Charlie tried hard to imagine what it would be like to travel the country playing jazz – and, wonder of wonders, getting paid to do it.

Later, inside, they would wave to acquaintances and check carefully – as everyone did – to see if they could spot anyone they knew up in the expensive 'royal boxes'. There would be time to study the printed programme, and then they would cock their heads to catch the tuning-up of the brass instruments, coming from behind the heavy curtains. Perhaps they would catch the thrilling little splash of a hi-hat cymbal, or the belligerent clump of a bass-drum pedal, as the drummer fussed around his kit making last-minute adjustments. The twinge of anticipation stiffened as the heavy, glittering chandeliers started to dim – dovetailing smoothly with the faltering babble of the good-humoured crowd as it settled down for the show. There was a heavy sliding noise from somewhere upstairs as the main spotlight threw a huge yellow circle down on to the velvet folds of the curtain. Now there was always a brief but unbearable delay, before the curtain swung upwards to reveal the band - already bursting into its signature tune. The first few bars were always inaudible – drowned in the enthusiastic roar of welcome. Charlie and Chris were floating: here were six youngish men up on stage who could bring to life their favourite recordings. The changing colours of the spotlights, the blurred fanning of drumsticks, the spinning gold of the cymbals, the choking and plaintive cries of muted brass and, not least, the smart, matching stage-suits of the band – all this was utterly intoxicating. Sometimes, a shimmering-gowned lady would be welcomed from the wings to sing some plaintive blues. The audience clapped till their hands were sore and cheered themselves hoarse. For the two schoolboys, the evenings flew away at a cruel speed. They never missed a Sunday concert.

On the way home from the Playhouse one night, Chris confided to Charlie that he'd been thinking of trying to start up a school jazz band. Who was available? They thought about it. There *was* a school orchestra of sorts: six violins, two 'cellos, two bassoons, a solitary trumpet and a pianist. They rehearsed excruciatingly under the baton of Miss Storer, a daunting senior mistress. Chris referred to them as the Abattoir All-Stars. He had, of course, once been an All-Star himself, and on the basis of this painful memory, now decided that only Noon, the pianist, was a possibility.

Mick Noon was a shy, sad-faced boy with lank brown hair which kept flopping down over his eyes. He always accompanied the daily hymns at assembly and had passed all his piano grades with distinction. This achievement qualified him as one of the privileged few who were allowed within five yards of the school's most majestic possession – the gleaming Bechstein concert-grand.

Chris said he would sound him out. He would have a word with Shore too, who was reported to be useful on the guitar but, more importantly, owned a banjo as well. Shore was, in fact, repeating most of his O-levels, after notching up an impressive string of failures earlier that summer. In appearance, he was on the small side: slim, with a pinkish complexion and wavy blond hair which he kept neatly combed. His eyes were a very pale-blue and his brows seemed always to be raised. As a result, he carried around with him a permanent expression of surprise. Unusually – for a schoolboy – he was fastidious about his blazer and flannels: they were pressed and clean; his tie was free from creases and soup stains; and he had been known to wear a dashing buttonhole. The male stereotype to which most of the boys aspired that year was a mixture of James Dean and

Tony Curtis; Dave Shore, however, appeared content to tread the older, nobler path of Leslie Howard. Naturally, he was not popular with the other boys: they said he was 'too flash'; they watched his daily performance with a contempt which clumsily disguised their secret envy. But *he* seemed oblivious, and it certainly did nothing to wound his confidence or hamper his busy schedule. He was a smooth talker and a charmer of surprising maturity and invention, who was to be seen holding hands with various girls on the school buses. The girls, too, had their own emphatic views about him: they claimed he was too conceited; that he was very selfish and totally unreliable; that he was *certainly* too saucy. These critics could be seen with him in the local coffee bar – only hours later – with their arms wrapped around his waist, their eyes gazing into his.

None of that was important, said Chris, as long as he could play banjo like Johnny St Cyr or Lawrence Marrero. Nor did it matter that he'd never been near *one* of the record recitals over the year – he could soon be drilled into shape.

The next morning, overtures were duly made to Mick Noon, who was signed up at once – protesting modestly from behind his lank hair that he knew nothing of jazz. Chris then went looking for Shore, who was usually to be found at the gate which separated the girls' quadrangle from the boys'. Sure enough, three of the slinkier temptresses were slouched up against the iron bars, quietly feasting upon some brand-new line from the charmer's apparently bottom-less store.

Shore quickly became 'Dave' as Chris outlined his proposal, while making sure, too, that the three girls could hear the conversation. Charlie calculated that his friend's reasons for doing this were twofold: first, the smoothy at the gate would be flattered – it would do his image no harm at all to accept (and Chris would have got his banjoist); secondly, wouldn't Chris have improved his *own* prospects with the girls by turning on this casual display of leadership?

Charlie looked on wistfully as the agreement was struck. He wanted to be included more than anything – but realized that such hopes were futile. The only musical instrument he had ever tried was the recorder, years before, at junior school. Top jazz players on that instrument were probably rare. He remembered his most recent music exam which had grossed him no better than a humiliating seven per cent. It was clear that he should resign himself to the role of loyal listener and abandon any thoughts involving performance. And his frustration was only agitated further by a recent suspicion that musicians got more – and better – girls than ordinary people did. Charlie had never had *any* girls. He played football for the First XI, and he usually won the art prizes – but those achievements seemed to count for nothing. The situation was tormenting, the outlook dismal.

And so Chris got his first little band together: the clarinet taking care of the melodies; the two new recruits providing the accompaniment. Practice sessions were held privately, and Charlie's job, as 'minder', was to turn away all inquisitive gatecrashers from the door of whichever classroom they'd been given permission to use. However, Chris always permitted two or three of Shore's ladies to attend. It was the most sensible idea, he said, for Shore would not be able to concentrate on mere music for more than five minutes at a stretch without some female stimuli. This little psychological ploy paid dividends, for although Shore now adopted an infuriatingly languid pose – redolent of an amused dilettantism – it was nevertheless obvious to everyone that he could play the banjo with a lot of flair. Mick, on the other hand, was more of a plodder – but scrupulously accurate. Chris was pleased and having fun; so too were the female camp-followers.

As for Charlie, he acted enthusiastically on the surface and made complimentary noises about the trio. Inwardly, he felt like a wretched underling, a musical fag. His seemed a light-weight role, an awkward position which lacked the social currency needed to land a dazzling girlfriend. He reminded himself, guiltily, of Chris's axiom: 'It's the music that counts', but dammit! – Chris had now got a regular girl; even old hymn-playing Mick had found one. So why couldn't he have one? What was worse, he knew the girl he wanted. He was secretly crazy about her, her green eyes, and about how she'd looked one day coming off the hockey pitch when the cold wind and driving rain had plastered her T-shirt against her breasts.

She was always at the practice sessions, but she ignored Charlie the doorman. Her name was Alice Gladwin.

The change in Charlie's fortunes came out of a purely casual remark.

'Rhythm's the thing we're missing,' said Chris one day as he adjusted his reed, squinting across the top of the mouthpiece. 'What we really need now is something to lay the beat down more strongly.'

The school could boast no percussionist and the only thing remotely usable was a huge ceremonial bass drum which had once belonged to the Combined Cadet Force. A tattered grey cord hung from it and the original paint was now badly chipped and scored. The skin had long since disappeared and the drum's only current use was as a substitute for stumps during impromptu games of indoor cricket.

That night, while walking up the steep lane which ran from the bus stop to his home, Charlie had the germ of an idea. To help develop it, he tried to picture the inside of his parents' garden shed. He was thinking of something he'd seen in there – but paid no attention to – when he'd been giving the lawns their final autumn crop, weeks before.

Nearing the house, he quickened his pace and trotted up the path – ignoring his pet collie, which was wagging and grinning in expectation of hugs and pats. He went straight to the shed and pulled open the wooden door, letting in a greyish wedge of light. Then he pushed the vintage mower out of the way and clambered over a bucket and a row of tins containing brushes, all of them congealed with the remains of old paint. He peered into the gloom. There it was – hanging from a nail on the back wall: an old-fashioned washboard with thick and twisted cobwebs in the corners of its wooden frame; the dark and light corrugations from its zinc working-surface were just perceptible in the half-light; it looked like a tiny patch of desert sand. The stencilled letters of the original manufacturer's name had faded away to a sad, pale grey – victims of detergent, water and time.

Charlie felt as exultant as Howard Carter at the Valley of the Kings. Standing there, with the spiders for company in the quiet mustiness of the shed, he gazed up at the simple gadget. Then, stretching on tiptoe over an old tea chest, he gently lowered his treasure from the wall. *Here* was the rhythmic beat Chris was searching for. *Here* was his passport to glamour and respect, and perhaps to Alice Gladwin.

All he needed now was thimbles, and he could be Chris's rhythm man, keeping time on the washboard like the musicians in the old jug bands.

He took it outside into the light and brushed away the cobwebs. It was still in decent condition. His mother was peering out of the kitchen window, and he turned towards her.

'Look at this!' he yelled.

The door opened and she came out. 'Where did you find that?' she asked, taking it from him.

'At the back of the shed, hanging on a nail.'

She turned it over slowly, looking a little rueful and sad. 'They were terrible on your hands, these things – I used to end up with red-raw knuckles; but they did the job, I suppose.'

'When did *you* use this, then?' asked Charlie.

'Oh . . . when you were both tots – during the war, when your dad was away.' She gave a sniffy little laugh. 'Well, no point in hanging on to old rubbish . . . might as well chuck it out.'

'*Chuck it out?*' spluttered Charlie. '*No fear!*'

Late that evening, he sat in pyjamas on the end of his bed; the freshly scrubbed and disinfected board was across his knee. On the ends of his fingers were jammed the tiny steel thimbles, pilfered from his mother's sewing-box. They were so tight that his nails were going numb while the rest of his hand became hot and flushed. He hardly noticed, and scraped away, trying to develop what he hoped would be an innovative technique. He started to sing softly:

Mah woman done left me; left me all alone.
Ah said mah woman done left me; she left me all alone.
Ah'd love to rock you baby, but baby, you done gone.

He was well into the second chorus of his home-made blues – and just adding a little fortissimo clatter with the thimbles – when his father rapped sharply on the door.
'FOR GOD'S SAKE SHUT THAT ROW UP! WE'RE TRYING TO SLEEP, AND YOU'VE GOT A PAPER ROUND TO DO AT SEVEN IN THE MORNING!'
'And don't forget to brush your teeth,' added his mother shrilly.
Charlie groaned to himself. What bloody Philistines! He switched off his light and climbed into bed. Through the thin wall, he could hear his sister sniggering ruthlessly in her bedroom.

Getting a washboard from A to B – by public transport – would not normally pose much of a problem, but next morning Charlie felt that a lot was at stake. With a place in Chris's band now waiting for him (and the delicious Alice possibly now his for the taking), he was determined to avoid any chance of an early humiliation at the hands of 'dunces'; for while his own belief in the washboard – as a valid musical instrument – was total, he was nevertheless keenly aware that the uninitiated would prove harder to convince. He wanted to avoid any inroads being made into his self-esteem before he even got the thing to school – and so he evolved a plan.

His solution was to wrap the board in heavy brown paper and secure it with plenty of string. Then he scrawled across the parcel in heavy black crayon: 'PHOTOGRAPHS: DO NOT BEND'. In this way, he prudently eased his chosen instrument into the world. All went well, and he congratulated himself on not risking a flashy entrance as he safely entered the school gates. He deposited the parcel at the secretary's office – 'to be collected' – and rushed off to a geometry class, rattling a pocketful of thimbles.

At lunchtime, Chris was looking cheerful and expectant as the gang gathered for the unwrapping. Alice was there and this set Charlie's heart bumping faster, for she was showing some curiosity too. Shore, meanwhile, was sitting, banjo in one hand, casually stroking the back of a girl's neck with the other. How typical of the sex-crazed bastard, fumed Charlie, as he picked away at the knots in the string. They came loose and he put his hand inside the brown paper. Then, taking a deep breath, he brandished the washboard above his head. There was silence, and they all stared hard. Chris's eyes lit up, but before he could speak, a long and derisive cackle of laughter rang out, unmistakably feminine, unquestionably Alice.

Charlie's head dropped, and he felt himself blush deeply – his hopes torpedoed by the very person he'd most wanted to impress.

Shore and his entourage were chuckling like drains, but Chris came to the rescue: 'Heh! Just a minute, you lot! You mean to say that *nobody* here knows about the washboard's place in jazz?'

There was a general shaking of heads as he took the board and held it up like a courtroom exhibit.

'I've played you Big Bill Broonzy records at our sessions, haven't I?'

Everyone nodded as Chris swept on, 'Well then – a lot of those country blues tracks had washboard players on them; in fact, Broonzy's own brother-in-law was Washboard Sam who recorded on the old Bluebird label. So you see, this instrument has an important history *and* don't forget both Louis Armstrong and Johnny Dodds recorded with one – and so it's nothing to laugh about.'

He looked round to a crimson-faced, but grateful Charlie: 'Have you got the thimbles to go with this? Great! OK, let's see what it sounds like.'

A suitable chair was dragged over and the gang fell respectfully silent. Chris waited a few moments for Shore, who was combing his hair in the reflection of the window, before snapping his fingers impatiently. 'OK ... when you're ready, Dave. We'll try a nice, medium-tempo blues. It'll give Charlie a chance to sort himself out; he'll get the feel. I'll beat it in – usual key – B flat.'

Charlie quickly jammed on the thimbles as one of the leader's heavy brogues slammed violently up and down on the parquet floor to establish a common tempo. The new quartet staggered away into the blues and at once Charlie felt provocatively adrift in a sea of panic and perspiration. He knew he was on trial; this was *it*; he had to prove that his voluntary contribution was worthwhile, and would benefit the others. His dreamy bedroom scraping had not prepared him for the real thing. The merciless metallic clank of the banjo in one ear and the dark rumbling piano in the other were inducing paralysis. Above the harmonic rumpus he was aware of the clarinet climbing into the upper register; he was sure it was angry about something.

Dazed and confused, he looked down and saw his own hands twitching and tapping in a desultory way. Chris's last order had been to 'keep it steady and simple'. Pulling himself together a little, he tried to identify the regular beat. He tried one sturdy, curving scrape across the board with the right-hand thimbles, followed by a sharp tap with the left – on alternate beats of the bar – and he thought that he might have something. He concentrated furiously upon this for a couple of choruses and it seemed to make some sort of sense. Although it was already dawning on him fast that his chosen instrument had severe limitations, he was nevertheless sure that his little rhythmic pattern was helping to tidy up the general sound, to knit it together. It was as if a huge pyjama-cord had been pulled tight and tied. With mounting excitement, he started to experiment with a few beefily syncopated taps and occasional bursts of extravagant scraping.

By the twelfth chorus the thimbles were heating up nicely. By the eighteenth they were red-hot and his forearms were aching and as heavy as lead. He dared to look up from the zinc for a moment at the encouraging sight of a row of shoes all tapping in time, like synchronized components of a loom. He steeled himself for the home straight, hoping that his anvil-arms would last the distance. Mercifully, Chris soon brought everything to a halt and there was an amused but complimentary cheer from the gang. Shore winked across and said, 'Nice stuff.' Charlie was taken aback by this, but conceded quietly to himself that Shore, after all, was probably OK – his attitudes had perhaps been misunderstood; he might be a tiny bit flashy, but he knew his music . . . no doubt there.

Chris walked over with a huge and generous grin on his face and he spoke the words Charlie desperately wanted to hear: 'Bloody marvellous, mate – you were really getting into it at the end. Oh . . . and welcome to the band!'

The bell was now clanging at the far end of the school and everybody started to move out to their classes. Charlie gathered up the brown wrapping-paper and stuffed it into a waste bin, then strode out into the corridor with the washboard proudly under his arm, for all to see. The thimbles were in his back pocket, cooling quickly. Alice had nipped away, but others smiled their congratulations.

He and Chris marched off – to geography and physics respectively – as equals.

The Christmas dance was now only hours away and everybody went home to change. The school's strict codes of dress were always relaxed a little for this one evening.

The annual metamorphosis achieved by the girls was staggering. Curves and cleavages were produced from out of nowhere, and by the most unlikely and humdrum of them. This, together with the girls' cunning application of make-up and alterations of hairstyles, induced in the unsuspecting boys (and some members of staff) an acute disorientation.

But with very few exceptions, the boys' parallel attempts at transformation failed pathetically. That sought-after goal of sophistication eluded generations of them, year after year.

Charlie, for instance, had tried especially hard. Two years earlier, an incredibly wide satin tie, featuring a hand-painted nude, had failed to impress, but *had* earned him a double detention mark – despite his plaintive explanation that it was a gift from an uncle in America. Another time, a bow tie which lit up and revolved at speed did manage to get him a few laughs – but no girls. He tried extra Brylcreem; then no Brylcreem. Once he planned to have longer hair and was shattered when his mother forced him to the barber's shop only two days before the dance. He'd once worn one of his father's jackets and this had augured well, for the shoulders were heavily padded and made him look, he thought, a bit like Jack Palance. Unfortunately, by the time he got to the dance the padding had started to sag over the bony ends of his own narrow shoulders, so that he resembled the roof of a Dutch town house.

Waistcoats, watch chains, pitiable moustaches . . . it was no use: whatever was tried, the boys could not escape from their pimply adolescence.

It was not easy to hang decorations in the school hall: there was a shortage of terminals where the ends of coloured streamers could be secured and drawing-pins were forbidden, for they would have wrecked the mahogany rolls of honour. They settled instead for a large plastic Christmas tree, which was jammed into the memorial fireplace at one end of the hall. The tree was smothered with the usual paraphernalia and, as a finishing touch, school funds had purchased a very beautiful little fairy which stood on tiptoe on the topmost branch, waving a tiny wand. Because of its height, at least eighteen inches of the tree disappeared up the chimney, and so people wishing to admire the fairy had to step into the grate and twist their necks painfully upwards in order to catch a glimpse of her now grimy shoes. The festive picture was completed by a few pale balloons jammed through the wrought iron of the balcony and some garish streamers looped around the necks of the marble busts, joining them up all the way round the hall like the rope fences that attempt to protect village-green cricket squares.

Against this simple backcloth, the festivities were about to begin. Down one side of the hall sat an enormous line of chattering girls, and all the way along the opposite wall an equivalent number of awkward-looking boys. The sexes faced each other across no man's land, like primed infantry at Waterloo.

There had never been any live dance music on these occasions; instead, Crisp and Arkwright – two studious and reliable boys – were detailed to work the gramophone, taking it in turns to put on a series of heavy old records with brown labels and gold lettering. They were crouched dutifully at their machine as Miss Mycroft came up and handed them a list.

She then stepped theatrically out into the middle of the floor: 'Take your partners for a veleta,' she announced, at the same time making two giant arcs with her arms, like a referee ordering fighters to 'box on'.

Crisp sent the polite sounds of Harry Davidson's Old-time Dance Orchestra piping out from the tiny machine and, with only three minutes of music at their disposal, a straggly rank of males stood up and marched crookedly across the 'open ground'. After a flurry of self-conscious invitation the most coveted belles were hauled off, leaving a handful of indignant wallflowers to sit staring through the throng of dancers at the sullen abstainers on the other side. They were soon taken care of by the alert Miss Mycroft, who rounded up both sets of stragglers at great speed, pairing them off like a border collie working her sheep.

Foxtrots, waltzes and tangos all followed as Crisp and Arkwright slogged away in their corner. Meanwhile, the quartet stuck together (as much as the diligent Mycroft shepherding would allow). They were being kept too busy to be nervous and Chris, especially, was making a name for himself on the dance floor. The musical grace and timing which he applied with ease to the clarinet did not extend as far as his huge and dangerous brogues; they were the subject of much acid comment as several of his partners were to be seen hobbling and cursing their way back to the wall after each dance.

Couples swayed by, shouting to Charlie: 'When are you on?'; 'Is it true you're playing tonight?'; 'Should be a good laugh!'

During the progressive barn dance, he found himself swinging legs in unison with Mr Copson, of French. They had not seen eye to eye on most matters over the previous four years – especially French.

'Understand you're going to entertain us shortly, Dunnicliff?'

'That's right, sir. Don't know it if will be any good though,' replied Charlie – deciding to take out a little insurance.

'We shall soon see,' called the master with a cold smile.

Later, during a brisk quickstep, the shiny and diminutive Dr

B Flat, Bebop, Scat

Chatterton of divinity came spinning up the hall, firmly locked in the arms of the strapping PE mistress. As they negotiated a corner the doctor managed to gasp: 'When's this cabaret of yours coming up, Dunnicliff?'

Before Charlie could answer, Miss Dawkes had the doctor accelerating in reverse along the back straight and down towards the tricky fireplace bend where, at their speed, great teamwork would be required if they were to avoid disaster.

So far, Charlie had not managed to dance with Alice. He'd been beaten to it each time – mostly by Bestwick, who was a very pushy character, bordering on loutish.

Charlie was stewing over this little annoyance when Miss Mycroft arrived at Chris's elbow: 'Well Bland, shall we be thinking of getting your little offering out of the way soon?'

'Oh . . . right, miss.'

'Yes, now let me think – coffee and biscuits are due to be brought in at ten. You know Bland, I think that would be as good a time as any for you.'

'Sounds all right to me,' agreed Chris.

'Very well . . . it's nearly a quarter to ten and so I suggest you all go and get your *instruments* ready,' she said, putting emphasis on the word and at the same time looking straight at Charlie. 'Presumably you have to *prepare* yourselves,' she added slyly.

Charlie felt a twinge of self-doubt. He was sure she'd been poking fun at him and his lowly washboard. Come to think of it – why had she agreed to let them perform anyhow? She was certainly a traditionalist, but *her* brand extended only as far as the 'classics' and tweed skirts from Scotland – not to jazz. Perhaps she was smugly anticipating a musical catastrophe; after all, it was often believed that public ridicule was as good a lesson as any for curing young people of empty ideas.

'Right lads, let's go and warm up,' said Chris. The four of them trooped out of the noisy hall into the dark chill of the quadrangle. As they left, Charlie was pained to see Alice dance by in the arms of the ruffian Bestwick. She was laughing, and he was peering intently down the front of her dress like a greedy child inspecting the contents of a narrow Christmas stocking.

'I didn't like the way she said we should be getting our offering "out of the way", did you, Chris?' asked Charlie when they reached the practice room.

'Yeh, I heard that.'

'She'd really love it if we fucked the whole thing up.'

'There's nothing she'd like more,' said the leader. 'But we're not going to, are we?' And with that, he took out his clarinet and ripped off a few confident phrases. Shore was meticulously tuning up, while Mick ran through some fast arpeggios at the little upright piano in the corner. Charlie felt a bit obsolete at warm-up time. He tried a bit of finger-stretching, then nervously counted his thimbles. Inside the room, the atmosphere was electric; outside, they could hear the elderly kitchen-ladies as they picked their way through the darkness towards the hall, wheeling trollies laden with coffee and crockery.

The door opened and a messenger from the hall said: 'They're waiting for you.'

The quartet moved out into the night air. They passed the locker rooms in mute single file, regrouping at the big swing doors leading into the main hall. Charlie bent forward and put his eye to the keyhole. He could see a long slice of the merrymakers quite clearly, sitting in little cliques now, holding cups and saucers. The recorded dance music had stopped; in its place a hum of expectancy. They would have to walk through all these people to get to the Bechstein at the far end of the hall.

'OK lads?' said Chris, and they pushed through the doors and into the arena like footballers appearing from the throat of Wembley Stadium.

' 'Ere they are!' shouted someone, and there was a festive cheer. The leader sloped his way across the floor and nodded good-naturedly to various friends, as if he had not seen them for some months, instead of twenty minutes ago. They noticed their own little bunch of partisans, all cheering wildly, and were waving back to them when Bestwick started shouting loudly: 'Eh! Eh! Look at Dunnicliff! Look what Dunnicliff's got under 'is arm!'

Every person in the room craned their necks to see. As more and more people realized what it was, a great wave of laughter crashed in on Charlie. He felt very silly and very angry – like a man who has lost his toupee in a gale.

As the noise subsided, Bestwick howled once more: 'Can you do me a vest, and a pair of pants while yer at it?'

This time, the laughter was long and lingering, from the bellies of both staff and pupils. Miss Mycroft, Mr Copson and a couple of other academic foes were enjoying this unexpected sport – a pleasant bonus, making this tedious, but obligatory evening with the Sixth just that little bit more bearable.

The crowd now sensed that they were going to enjoy themselves and dragged their chairs forward to make sure of a good view – so that the musicians were soon completely hemmed in by a horseshoe of grinning faces. Bestwick, exhilarated by the success of his heckling, had moved up alongside the piano to be in a good position

to add any further gems that might occur to him.

Chris sensed that this comic interlude was in danger of altogether ruining the short concert, and he was anxious to start. He looked inquiringly at the other three; Charlie plunged his hand into his pocket for his thimbles and realized, with absolute horror, that he'd left them in the practice room. He leapt to his feet, shoved through the startled crowd and sprinted down the hall. As he ran, he heard Bestwick's raucous voice once more: ' *'E's forgot 'is music!'*

The place erupted again and it was obvious that the crowd was fast adopting Bestwick as an extra turn.

A breathless and sweating Charlie reappeared and took his seat, careful to avoid the thundery expression on Chris's face. He started to jam the thimbles on to his fingers and Bestwick attempted another personal triumph – something about a hole in his sock.

'OK, OK, start . . . *start!*' hissed Charlie.

Chris turned away and nodded to Miss Mycroft, who stepped forward to address the crowd: 'Ladies and gentlemen! Tonight we are in for something special . . . well . . . certainly something *different!*'

At this, George Pope, the affable woodwork master, let out a cheerful squawk and pointed at Charlie's washboard. The whole place collapsed, yet again.

'Quiet please! . . . Now, quiet please!' shouted a delighted Miss Mycroft, waving a playful finger of admonition at her colleague. 'Tonight, you are to be entertained by four of your fellow students: Christopher Bland, Michael Noon, David Shore, and Charles Dunnicliff, who are going to play a selection of jazz music for you.' There were a few cheers. She had pronounced the word 'jazz' with the enthusiasm generally accorded to words like 'taxation', or 'haemorrhoids', but went on: 'As it is the very first time we have been honoured with live *cabaret* at one of our functions, I think an encouraging hand would be appropriate.'

The ensuing enthusiastic applause helped calm Charlie as he struggled to get the final thimble on to the fourth finger of his right hand. This was especially tricky, as every finger of his other hand was already wrapped in steel. The applause died away.

'Pray silence for the artistes,' whispered Miss Mycroft as she stepped back, beaming, into the audience.

'Piss artists, more like,' said Bestwick in a stage whisper, causing several of his new fans to hold their sides in agony, their faces screwed up in paroxysms of pleasure.

Chris put the clarinet to his mouth and was about to beat in the tune when the silence was broken by a thin, metallic bouncing sound, which quickly became a gentle trickle of steel as Charlie's problem thimble disappeared under the concert-grand. He looked up hopelessly at Chris and then slithered down off his chair. The latest reaction of the crowd would have guaranteed them a month at the Palladium – if they had been a comedy act.

He located the thimble under the nine-foot Bechstein and would have been happy to stay down there, anonymous in the gloom, for the rest of his life. However, he took a deep breath, wiped his brow on his sleeve, pressed the thimble securely on to his finger and crawled out to another great cheer. This broke into more guffaws as he straightened up too soon and gave his head a resounding crack. By this time, even Chris had been forced to smile. His greeting of his emergent friend – 'Miff the Mole, I presume?' – was not appreciated by the victim.

At last the mighty brogue thundered down and the four of them went off at a furious pace. Charlie put his head down and seemed to be attempting a wild finger-exorcism. It was as if he was trying to scrape the tension and humiliation right out of himself. For a few minutes, the washboard was returned to its original purpose: of cleansing, of scrubbing and scouring and rasping out every blotch and stain left over from such an unnerving experience. He smashed his way across the zinc, doing anything that came into his head. He didn't care any more whether they liked it or not and when he heard Chris's familiar finishing phrase coming up, he decided that he'd add an extra eight bars of solo percussion on to the end – just for the hell of it. Chris caught on to the idea and came in with a dazzling burst of notes to round it all off. The other two had been listening closely too, and although nothing like that had been rehearsed before, they finished together, perfectly.

There was a stunned silence and then the place exploded. A great volley of noise slapped them in the face. Everyone was on their feet – clapping and whooping delightedly. Chris was standing with his arm outstretched, diverting the applause in Charlie's direction and motioning him to stand and take a special bow. He rose, feeling slightly drunk, and gave a dubious little wave of the washboard. It was some time before they could carry on.

It may have been that the crowd felt guilty for having enjoyed themselves so much at Charlie's expense earlier on; whatever it was, he could do no wrong. Encores were demanded and they could probably have gone on all night if Miss Mycroft had not stepped in, instructing Crisp and Arkwright to get cracking again. Soon Jimmy Shand and his band were banging out a Scottish reel and the infantry were back in position along the walls. Bestwick drifted away, looking puzzled.

The boys were rejoined by their delighted gang, and congratula-

tions poured in from all sides. The term was about to end and there
was only one sad note: they would have to wait until the New Year
before taking their musical plans further.

Charlie had been badly rattled for most of the evening, but as he
walked out of the school in the December darkness, with the dew
turning shiny on the ground, he felt more stimulated than ever
before. He had tasted a drug and he was hooked.

People were still shouting happy goodnights and he headed off to
catch the last bus home. As he passed the girls' entrance-gate, a soft
voice called his name from the shadows and a figure slipped out and
took his arm. It was Alice.

'I just wanted to say sorry for laughing that time, and that you were
all really great tonight. You should have seen old Mycroft's face at
the end – it was a picture!'

'Oh . . . thanks,' stumbled Charlie, 'thanks very much, but . . . er
. . . aren't you with Bestwick?'

Alice looked aghast – 'What? . . . Me, with *that* creep?'

They stayed together on the bus all the way to her village. Then he
walked the three miles back through the frosty moonlight with his
washboard under his arm. He knew he had never felt happier.

Sleep was impossible. The sound of applause still hummed in his
head, competing there with the debilitating memory of Alice's
wonderful goodnight kisses. His favourite image of her – playing
hockey in the rain – came back for the umpteenth time. He switched
the light back on and reached for his beloved board:

If I could be with you for just one hour tonight,
If I could say and do all those things I might,
I want you to know, that –

There was an angry outburst from the bottom of the stairs:
'CHARLES! WILL YOU PLEASE SHUT UP AND PUT THAN DAMN
THING AWAY? DON'T YOU REALIZE THE TIME, FOR GOD'S
SAKE?'

A malicious sisterly snigger filtered through from the next room,
and as he slipped across the landing to go to the bathroom,
concerned voices were drifting softly up the stairs: 'Damned
ridiculous! We move heaven and earth to get him into a good school,
and what happens? He ends up scraping a blasted washing-board!
Some future in that!'

Charlie turned off his light and smiled the contented smile of a
liberal and tolerant artiste: 'Plebs,' he thought, 'but well-meaning
enough.' He decided it was best to wait until after the holidays to
review his musical career. It was also a bit too early to consider

changing his name – but Washboard Charlie did have an authentic and agreeable lilt to it. He would have to think it over.

In Memoriam Mingus (1922 – 79)

Elaine Cohen

Mingus ah um – when you were a little
bowlegged fat kid draggin' that cello around
and your shoeshine box on chicken legs – bumped
into Buddy Collette who took you down to the
Million Dollar Theatre to hear Red Callender
'the cat that's gettin' the sound, man . . .'

you knew, at 17, it'd take 18
hours a day practising bass
on the hot front porch off Central Avenue
to get them 4 and 9 no bar lines
misunderstood Mingus fingers in yr soul

Then – bye bye porkpie – far from LA
Dizzy moods met irascible Charles
   shooting arrows at egg yolks
   on the sidewalks of New York
  wolfing 4 steaks at a sitting
   Pithecanthropus Erectus
urging unguent beauty on the Workshop
'Don't play notes! Play yourself!'
   voracious rage boiling
   teeth flying
   thrice upon a theme
   fight song/table dance
   and all the things you C sharp

B Flat, Bebop, Scat

But that day at Monterey you didn't blow your top
the musicians kept their chops and you were like
a great genie presiding . . . 'Preach! Preach! Pray!'
telling fables of Faubus, integrating meditations
writing open letters to Duke for all the world
dreaming 'they' were against you, 'they' were
coming to get you . . . Cry for Freedom!

Orange dress, blue sky, slivered
silver lining – that jello feel
    in your body when Buddy hugged you
weird Mexican nightmare
    where vultures hovered on cue
The chill of death was awful
you sat in your wheelchair
paralysed, slathered with cakes of cow dung
stuffed with snails and tortillas
you – reincarnation of a lovebird
what love
tears dripped down your cheeks
Couldn't talk . . . crooked a finger as if to say
'I'm going to play again'
Bird called
and your ashes dissolved
on the Ganges

The Killers of '59

Digby Fairweather

Digby Fairweather, having lived jazz music for at least thirty-seven of his thirty-nine years, feels that this should have equipped him to play cornet like Bobby Hackett and/or to write like Tom Sharpe. But he notes ruefully that neither is the case. His story, however, is a factual portrayal of some of the nastier levels of 1950s dance-band life.

For the audition, the examiner had set a single chair and a music stand with a sheet of music on it in the centre of the recording studio. To reach the chair the examinee must walk six paces across thick carpet, his footsteps padding flatly back from the thick curtain drapes that lined the walls.

The trumpeter unclipped the catches on his leather case and with deliberately slow movements removed a heavy trumpet and weathered mouthpiece. The mouthpiece dropped with a 'tenk' into the trumpet shank, and the trumpeter, after securing it, moved into a corner and began – still unhurriedly – to blow warm-up exercises into the curtains.

The men behind the glass panel watched him from above. An engineer opened a microphone and the warm sound of controlled ascending diminished arpeggios filled the booth. The reactions from the listeners were varied. The engineer nodded interrogatively to a portly silver-haired man in a fur-collared coat, who stood nearby. The portly man smiled warmly back. His colleague – a thinner, dark man with a hairline moustache – simply stiffened slightly and leant forward on his stool, peering into the glass tank through a pair of half-lens pince-nez.

Down in the studio the intercom ticked. 'I think we're ready for you when you're ready for us,' advised the engineer, in a tone that was carefully easy. The trumpet player – small, with a mop of Beatle-cut hair – turned slowly, and looked up nodding. Then he made the six-pace walk to the chair and sat down. The title of the music read 'Well, Git It', and opened up into six pages; a lead trumpeter's transcription of the Tommy Dorsey *tour de force*, followed by the combined solos of Charlie Shavers and Ziggy Elman painstakingly recopied. The trumpeter scanned the open pages, but beyond the flicker of an eyebrow, his expression did not alter.

The intercom ticked. This time it was the bespectacled man who leaned over to talk back. 'Give me your tempo,' he said, and the trumpet player, after glancing at the head of the music, considered, and then counted a brisk, steady '1-2-3-4-' into the microphone.

The bespectacled man reached to the mixing desk and grasped a metronome which he set, with cocked head, exactly to the trumpeter's beat. Then slowly he reached for the talkback button again. 'I'll give you the four,' he said steadily to the seated figure below. 'Then you're on your own.'

A hand waved in response. The bespectacled man, without saying more, picked up a copy of the score and recounted four with the metronome, into the talkback. The response from the trumpet was challenging. The lead line came up from below, clear and centred, every inflection and dynamic marked and observed, undeviant from the click of the metronome. From the clean and straight interpretation of the lead-trumpet part, the performer moved on to the transcribed solos of Shavers and Elman, with their looser rhythm and stronger vibrato. At one slippery phrase, executed with *fraulich* accuracy, the thin man allowed himself the ghost of a smile, but it was quick to fade. At last the one-man duet drew to an end, climbing at the last note to a super G, achieved with a trace of confident overhang, and a bellicose, full-throated shake. The metronome ticked on undisturbed into the silence, while the fur-collared man smiled approval through the glass, and – with a questioning eyebrow – towards his thin colleague. Then, with only a nodded response for guidance, he pressed the talkback button. 'Thank you very much,' he said. 'Would you come up please?'

The trumpeter got up slowly, plotted his way to the control booth with his eyes, and walked deliberately to the staircase. As he entered, the fur-collared man stepped slowly forward to shake his hand. 'You sound very good,' he said. 'And I think, if Manny agrees, we should try you out for the Blackpool week. On lead. It's our usual June week at the Tower, with a live broadcast on "Show Band Time" on Thursday.'

The trumpeter smiled and nodded. 'Fine – thank you, Mr Hall,' he said softly.

The fur-collared man smiled back and indicated his companion. 'This is Manny Kemp,' he said. 'Manny is our second trumpeter – and my second-in-command. He'll take care of you.'

The trumpeter looked across to see the thin man watching him keenly from behind the pince-nez. He smiled uncertainly and received in response a slow acknowledging nod. 'Yes, Mr Hall,' said Manny. And with a regal wave Tommy Hall, broadcasting bandleader, made his considered exit.

The thin man surveyed the young trumpeter appraisingly. 'That was fine playing,' he observed. 'I always loved Elman; the king of trumpet players!' There was a pause, and then a sharp question. 'How's your jazz? Your busking if you prefer.'

The trumpet player made a self-deprecatory gesture.

'Ah well,' said Manny. 'We'll have to see. Meantime, I suppose you could use a drink?'

The trumpeter was about to say, 'I don't really drink . . .' but he was waved aside. 'Some of the men should be in the bar by now,' said Manny. 'They'll be waiting to see their new leader. *And* drink with him, *capisci?*'

There was a moment's pause in which the trumpeter glanced curiously at Manny and was met by an unflinching gaze. Then he nodded in silent agreement.

'A large one then,' said Manny. 'To celebrate. We're buying.'

It was three hours later, in the King's Head, that the first ripples disturbed the water.

Around the table sat the trumpeter, in a mild haze but still alert, Manny, and two other trumpeters from his brass section: Stan Priddick – middle-aged, deftly garrulous, and with quicksilver reactions – and Tom Ball, who sat silently, a noncommittal listener.

Manny was talking. 'So it was Liverpool, eh?' He looked across at the trumpeter. 'You must have known the Empire then?'

'I did,' said the trumpeter. 'Saw *you* there lots of times too. The first time was the concert with Chet Baker – the one where he just sang.'

'Best thing he could do, darlin',' said Priddick swiftly. 'Or maybe the *only* thing! That union ban was lucky for him! After all, you know, I mean he never could really play. Not what we call *play*. He had a few licks – you know, his own little licks. But that was all. And he knew it! Came up to Tom here and said, "I'm gonna leave all that hard work to you." Didn't he, Tom? Ah-ha-a-ah! And he was right.

Tommy would have eaten him.'

The new arrival smiled but made no comment.

Manny – ever watchful – stiffened slightly.

'Of course, we all know about Chet Baker,' he said. 'But I never heard you play before.' He looked across the table at the trumpeter. 'That's a shame. How did I miss you?'

'I did cornet in Wigan Brass Band,' said the new colleague. 'Then it was solo cornet for five years. After that I played for the Liverpool Big Band – lead. We had a Sunday-morning season down at the Cavern Club. Where that new group the Beatles started up.' There was a pause.

'Well, how fortunate *that* doesn't seem to have done you any fucking harm, dear boy,' said Ball with a cynical flicker. His colleagues laughed.

'I don't know,' said the trumpeter, slightly defensive. 'They had an incredible following . . . I never saw the club so packed. And they had some original things of their own that were great.'

The atmosphere around the table turned quickly to ice.

Then slowly and deliberately Manny spoke. 'We shan't talk about that,' he said, in a voice that cut through the bar gossip. 'I *suggest* we talk about *music* instead.'

The trumpeter glanced across and saw that behind the pince-nez Manny's eyes had narrowed to slits, as he leaned forward. 'So while you were listening to Chet Baker – and playing for the Beatles in the meantime – where did you learn about *jazz*?'

'Jazz was never my strong point,' admitted the trumpeter, avoiding the challenge. 'I always liked the sound of lead-trumpet players – Ferguson, Gozzo, Harry James.'

'And Bobby Pratt?' pursued his interrogator.

'Yes, of course, Bobby. And Dick Hawdon. Two of the greats.'

'I don't recall,' said Manny, slowly again, 'that Bobby ever had any difficulty playing jazz. Not at all. A very fine jazz player, Bob, and the best lead player, many people thought. Dick Hawdon too, for that matter. Most of the good lead players I know were great jazz players too. Ziggy Elman, Butterfield, and of course Harry James, who you say you like. Would you agree with my point?' His pince-nez gleamed, supporting the attack.

'Yes,' said the trumpeter carefully. 'But for me, playing lead's something different; a separate thing. I play the lead . . .' He paused and looked firmly across at Manny. 'And I leave the jazz to those who can do it. And don't work so hard. Lead's something else.'

There was a long pause while the two men sized each other up. Finally Manny, very slowly, and with a hard edge to his voice said simply: 'I don't agree with you.'

There was another pause while the two men's gazes locked. Then the trumpeter dropped his eyes. 'Well,' he said, 'either way I must be going. Want to look through the book for tomorrow.'

'Good idea,' said Priddick. 'See you on the green.'

'Tomorrow,' said Ball with a nod.

'And don't bring any Chet Baker licks with you,' added Manny with a stainless-steel twinkle. The trumpeter nodded and made his way to the door.

It was Manny who picked up the conversation. 'That young man,' he said quietly, 'has a lot left to learn.'

Just then a button on the juke box keyed the sound of the Beatles into the smokey room. It was as if the same button had cued Manny's reaction. It was violent. 'There,' he exploded, his walls of reserve dramatically flattened, '*that's* what we have to contend with! Neanderthal fucking man playing three chords on a Neanderthal fucking instrument that *used* to be great! Making a nonsense of our great heritage of jazz! Of the great statements of Armstrong, James and Elman! And *he* . . .' he nodded vehemently towards the door, '*he* says that jazz is for the lesser lights. Which of course, next door to *that*,' he swung his head towards the juke box, 'it must be.' For just a second Manny's fists were white around his glass. 'Well, my old friends,' he finished, emptying his whisky glass, 'we'll put some grey in that God-awful hairstyle of his! He'll need a strong nerve this week. Oh yes!'

'It's the new breed,' said Priddick compliantly. 'Of *course* things can't always be as they were. Times change, music changes.'

Manny shot him a threatening glance, and Priddick continued hurriedly, 'But it doesn't disappear altogether – just because of what's happening to a few Liverpool scouses.' He motioned towards the juke box. 'Everyone knows that . . .'

Manny held up a finger, and cut across him. 'I'm a musician – and a lead trumpeter too,' he said dangerously, 'in case you'd forgotten. Or should I say I *was* a lead trumpeter.'

There was a short uncomfortable pause. Then Manny continued. 'And this whole situation is a *test-case* my friends. *A test-case.* We're going to show Tommy Hall once and for all that you don't forget who the professionals are. Or who your mates are. And we'll show him that professional standards are not for compromising. Not like they do in *rehearsal bands*! In *Liverpool*!' He leant on the words with lead-heavy irony.

'That was how Bobby Pratt started, I thought,' said Ball. 'And look what happened to him.'

Manny looked up with dramatically raised eyebrows, stage-shrugged and walked back to the bar.

Tuesday night at the Tower Ballroom rang up just as the Tommy Hall Band Show rang up nightly. Hall walked to centre-stage in his powder-blue Italian suit to greet the crowds. Then, as he shot his cuffs and raised his arms, the curtains opened on to three ranks of immaculately combed hair, neat grey uniforms and gleaming horns making a fanfare of 'Say It with Music'.

For the new arrival it was an easy induction. The first three tunes passed with sparkling full-toned ease. Manny, one seat to his left, played steadily and unshiftingly, his trumpet pointed stoically ahead of him with only one indication, to begin with, that he was on the same stand as the young trumpeter. When one final full-toned top G from the newcomer capped the section and held on one half-second longer than Tommy Hall's downbeat allowed, Manny's trumpet bell flashed four inches to the right. It was a swift challenging rebuke, like a heavyweight champion's first punch to the ribs.

Now Tommy Hall walked to the single centre-stage microphone. 'Ladies and gentlemen,' he said, cuffs shooting like rockets. 'We'd like to introduce you to our fine new arrival. He's the baby of the band . . .' – there was an expectant move forward by two or three pretty girls at the audience's rim – 'and he's the newest Mersey sound of all. With the Tommy Dorsey classic "Well, Git It", please welcome . . .' The name was lost to all but the front rows as suddenly, unaccountably, the microphone went dead.

'Well, Git It' went as smoothly as the first time. The trumpeter moved from his lead position in the section to play once again the duel roles of Elman and Shavers. The sound of his trumpet rose easily over and above the section behind him and through the fireworks of the last chorus to an intense double high C at the coda. There was a roar of applause and the trumpeter – unguarded for a moment – swung towards his colleagues with a triumphant smile. Immediately he felt a chilly wind. Manny, without a look or a word, was turning the music up for the number twenty-eight, 'Robins and Roses', a vocal interlude by Dahlia Lay.

It was during the final bars of 'Robins and Roses' that the trumpeter, for the first time, became aware that the second-trumpet part was pushing intensively over the section as if daring him to play just a little louder. Once the imbalance prompted a quizzical look from Tommy Hall. Then, in the second half – during a 'Body and Soul' feature for Bob Efford – it happened again. Halfway through a closely written brass chorale the trumpeter found that trumpets two, three and four were combining in a fortissimo challenge to his lead. He determined to say nothing.

As the curtain came down, Manny turned with a smile as steely as his pince-nez. 'How are you feeling?' he asked. 'You have to be strong to keep up with the killers.' The trumpeter understood. 'Good work anyway. Now – we buy you a drink. You play with the killers! You drink with the killers!'

Warming up in the dressing-room next evening (blowing away the cobwebs, Manny called it) the trumpeter began to wonder if he had imagined the challenges of the night before. He was conscious too of some uncomfortable and unfamiliar lip-fatigue.

It was after 'Well, Git It' – more modestly received than the night before – that the trumpeter felt the same threats recurring. Halfway through 'Robins and Roses' the cup-muted force of the other three, studiously close to their microphone, forced him into an overblown overdrive once more. After one tiny mispitching he made as a result, Manny's second-trumpet part rose momentarily an annoyed octave above him. This time it was the trumpeter's bell that jerked reprovingly to the left and immediately Manny's note dropped back to its correct register like a cobra dropping back into a charmer's basket.

It was at the end of the second half that things began to go very wrong. 'At the Woodchopper's Ball' – not for once 'Say It with Music' – closed the evening. It was a Tommy Hall rearrangement of the Woody Herman original, and like most Tommy Hall rearrangements, suffered in comparison. Still, there was time for most of the clichéd, show-stopping devices: a marathon saxophone battle, spotlit drum solo, and an obligatory last ascension through four keys guaranteed to whip every last lip-muscle of the trumpet section into submission.

It was during this final assault that the trumpeter found – unaccountably – that his microphone had failed. And that once again the trumpet section, hunched over their microphones with furrowed brows, were raising the game to a unified ear-splitting battlecry. Against this, production of his high and testing lead line was feeling, by quick turns, arduous, almost impossible, and then impossible. As the sound expired in an inaudible rush of wind with ten bars to go, the trumpeter was aware that his written part – shakily, but with graceless speed – was taken up by the chair to his left.

As the curtain fell, he felt a hand on his shoulder. 'Tough luck,' said the glittering pince-nez as they hurried to the dressing-room. The trumpeter morosely disassembled his mute stand and followed on.

When he opened the door the conversation stopped quite

abruptly, but he had just time to hear Manny say, 'I don't know if it's going to work Tommy . . .' Tommy Hall nodded and left the room, pausing only to smile bemusedly at the trumpeter as he went.

Manny smiled too. 'Not to worry,' he said comfortably. 'Each and every one of us has nights that he'd prefer to forget. Let's not worry about teething problems, *capisci?*' He squeezed the trumpeter's arm. 'Now come on! buy you a large one. Just to calm your nerves.'

The next evening in the dressing-room, the trumpeter was conscious of two things – the bleary, unfocused sensation of a hangover, and what was worse, a dry and reluctant lip. Watching Manny's ostentatiously methodical preparations, he felt a flash of anger, controlled it, and spoke. 'There's one thing to watch. Manny? Everybody?' he said with unnatural speed. Manny and his three cohorts turned in apparently rehearsed unison and looked directly at him. 'Volume.'

'Oh,' said Manny slowly, and raised his eyebrows. 'Do you really think so?'

'Yes,' persisted the trumpeter. 'On the vocals yesterday for one thing. Some of the mezzos are coming out forte, and more. It happens a lot. It's not right – and it's attracting attention from the boss.'

Manny looked him up and down. 'I rather think,' he said with heavy irony, 'that Mr Hall *likes* his brass section to be heard. Or perhaps you don't know that!'

'Burman's Bauble, Burman's Bauble,' said Stan Priddick like clockwork. 'Burman's Bauble, there in the *Melody Maker* for, what was it Manny, the "killer brass team of 1959"?'

'The killer brass team of 1959,' repeated Manny, like a Black Litany. 'Ask Heath. Ask Dankworth. We *destroyed* Tommy Sampson and even you should know how hard *that* was. If, of course, they ever talked about *music* in Liverpool.' The pince-nez flashed sparks.

'Nevertheless,' said the trumpeter, ignoring the challenge. 'That's no reason to play what's written wrongly. You know that, Manny.'

There was a short pause.

'No,' said Manny. 'That is correct.' He waited again, then glanced fleetingly at his sidemen. 'More care gentlemen – when you think so. *Capisci?* Oh by the way,' he added, 'some very old friends are coming in tonight to listen to our music. You won't have met them – yet. They like to hear "At the Woodchopper's Ball", save them. So I've asked Tommy to put it in again. Somewhere at the end.' He smiled across.

Once on the stand the trumpeter knew at once that this was going to be a long night. His lip was in poor condition. Notes that should have felt easy felt reluctant, and those at the top and bottom of the trumpet register threatened to disappear without ceremony. The evening would have to be played his way, even if further confrontation was inevitable. Accordingly when 'Robins and Roses' once again threatened to boil over, he snatched a minim rest to hiss 'No,' along the section, and after an angry movement, the volume stayed low. Later, in 'Body and Soul', more welling volume had to be quelled by a 'hush' sent along the row of bowed heads. It seemed to work, and very slowly the end of the evening appeared on the horizon.

Tommy Hall was front of stage. 'Which brings us,' he was saying, 'to the end of our show. But before we go a special finale for our friends paying us a special visit tonight – "At the Woodchopper's Ball".'

The trumpet player began like a watchful sprinter entering the last lap. As the final ascension of the keys began, he shouted 'Watch it,' along the section, and heard the volume-level reluctantly modify. At the concluding chorus, with a triumphant dash he played the last fifteen top Fs to home at triple-forte. At the line he was suddenly aware that the race had been taken out of his hands. Manny, on his feet, was suddenly waving and shouting, 'Up again! Up again!' to Tommy Hall, who smiled assent, bowed, and waved back. The crowd roared. The music continued on and up, louder and louder, rising key by key, for – the trumpeter thought – four more choruses. His lip had not survived the first. Manny, on lead again, had lasted for two more, and the clarinettist had taken over for the last. As the curtain fell, Manny passed behind him like a speeding demon.

The trumpet player, as he put his trumpet away, tried to control his anger. Then he walked swiftly to the dressing-room, knowing whom he would find there. As he opened the door he heard Manny say, 'What did I tell you, Tom,' but again the conversation stopped abruptly.

Then Hall turned to the trumpeter. 'These are some old friends of the band,' he said, indicating six perspiring invaders. 'They remember that "never going to finish" routine on "Woodchopper's" so Manny suggested we put it in. I don't think we've used it since the Palladium concert!' He smiled forgivingly. 'You have to be prepared for anything with my bunch of hooligans. Now then! With all our friends here I'm going to break my rule for once. Let's all go for a drink.'

In the bar, Tommy Hall bought the first large scotch. The trumpet player – still simmering with anger, and strangely tired – bought the next. And after that, everyone lost count. Drinking steadily, the trumpeter watched himself become incoherently drunk, able only to observe that with every drink his colleagues seemed to move further into clear-eyed sobriety. Then a vague recollection of Manny guiding him to the door, saying something about 'broadcast tomorrow', then a half-remembered stumbling walk through dawning streets. Five hours of uneasy sleep, and a bleary awakening to garish morning light.

The trumpeter pulled himself out of bed and splashed his face with water. Then he plugged in the electric kettle for tea, and pulled on a pair of corduroy jeans. In was the moment at which he unclipped his trumpet case and pulled out the heavy instrument that the half-formed worry at the back of his mind clipped into focus too.

A quick foray through the bottom register was enough to convince him. His lip was bruised and raw, refusing to respond quickly to even the simplest of trumpet phrases. The trumpeter did what all good players do and put the trumpet down for ten worried minutes while he determinedly drank tea. On the return visit nothing had improved. His playing in the lower register sounded fluffy and approximate, in the upper, unnaturally loud and bright. Between the two there was a gap in which nothing very much was happening at all. Near to panic, the trumpeter went to the bathroom to empty a jugful of hot water through his instrument. Had some practical joker emptied an ashtray down the bell? The water came out discouragingly clean.

After an hour of nervously pacing the floor, the trumpet player reached a decision. He would go for just one drink and come back to sleep. A good long deep sleep, he was sure, would clear his head, tone up his body, and restore his system to the old order. So, a swift walk along the street and up the steps to the door of the King's Head.

In the bar he met Manny, Stan, and Tom, but after a few words, found it easy not to join them. And back again in the boarding-house he allowed himself an occasional luxury: two strong sleeping-pills. Then he changed into pyjamas and pulled the covers over his head.

Just as a warm, comforting oblivion spread through his system there came a persistent knock at the door. 'I'm sorry to bother you old man,' said Stan Priddick. 'Oh, did I *wake* you? Oh damn, I *am* sorry! I forgot you were going to rest. Manny asked me to remind you that there's a six o'clock call tonight. In the hall – to balance for the broadcast. Break a leg old lad! Oh look I *am* sorry! You go back and get your sleep! Go on now!'

B Flat, Bebop, Scat

The opening moments of the trumpeter's six o'clock soundcheck were the worst of his life. His lip was rustily immobile, and several trial-run passages played into a tin mute fizzled out in a fluff of air. There was nothing to do but report to his deputy. He did so.

'Oh,' said Manny, eyebrows raised. 'Some trouble?'

'Yes. Something's wrong. I must have gone at it too hard last night sometime.'

'I did wonder,' said Manny. 'And not just with the trumpet either. And what about when you knocked into Stan in the bar last night. That was unlucky! While you were playing for us.'

Now he remembered. 'Well, anyway – if I lean across, help.'

'I'll do my best,' said Manny levelly, 'but remember – I'm not a lead trumpeter. Any longer.' He leaned on the words. 'That's why you were hired.'

The trumpeter said nothing.

'I suppose,' pursued Manny, 'that "Well, Git It" will have to go?'

The trumpet player nodded.

'I'll see Tommy,' said Manny.

What was left of the strength in the trumpeter's lip was gone by selection three – 'Body and Soul' – in Tommy Hall's live broadcast. At the end of that one he had motioned to Manny to take over the last high bars, and Manny had – just – managed the job. Halfway through 'Apple Honey' it had been possible to drop the busy building trumpet figures by one full octave. But in the final choruses it was Manny who led the coda from top E to super G.

Tommy Hall, perspiring visibly, motioned the figures five and eight with his fingers. The trumpeter felt a sensation of panic. He had never seen this number in the book, and turned up the music with a feeling of forboding. The announcer was speaking.

Manny leaned across. 'Change of programme,' he whispered. 'Everything in order? Yes? No?'

The trumpet player saw the music and his mouth went dry. 'Over the Rainbow'. 'Trumpet One. Ballad Feature,' read the title. On the page were written sixteen lines of slow low-register legato trumpet music.

He turned back to Manny, sweat breaking out on his hands and forehead. 'I'm not sure . . .' he said faintly, and looked across to see the announcer silently waiting and Tommy Hall staring across in supplication.

Manny moved quickly and purposefully. 'Right,' he hissed. 'You stand up – go on – go on – I'll do it.' And while the trumpeter stood on shakey legs, with dark stains breaking out under the arms of his light-grey bandjacket, he soundlessly fingered the trumpet valves while Manny Kemp stooped low over his music stand and blew

'Over the Rainbow' into the trombone microphone, one level below.

The rest of the ten minutes passed in a speedy blur. The moment the red light snapped off the trumpeter reached for the bottle of whisky he had slipped in his pocket for a comforter, and took a long, masking drink. He knew there was no need to hurry for the dressing-room. When at last he opened the door, Manny and Tom were still seated, and Hall walked quickly past him and out of the room.

By the time Manny arrived in the King's Head, the trumpeter was sitting blearily by himself, several empty doubles glasses in front of him. Manny settled himself, lit a pipe, and took off his pince-nez. 'Well,' he said. 'I'm sorry! It seems, from what Mr Hall says, that we haven't found the answer yet. He thinks you need a few more years – so we have to let you go.'

The trumpet player looked dimly at him. At that moment Stan Priddick and Tom Ball settled themselves into the seats opposite, and in controlled unison pushed double whiskies across the table.

'Don't worry lad,' said Priddick. 'It's a very tough game this – and you have to get your wings. This is the first stage of getting your wings! I was just the same at your age.'

The trumpeter looked at him, and quite suddenly, drank the whisky down in one gulp.

'Francisco Cavez,' continued Priddick, 'Francisco, he said to me, "It's a lifetime's work getting one *note* right." Mind you – if you don't mind my saying so – you should be careful of that.' He motioned to the empty glasses. 'It's funny how that'll get hold of you, lad. I had an old pal once . . .'

The trumpet player was suddenly aware that all three of his drinking companions had slipped out of focus. Priddick's voice rattled on from somewhere in a distant echo-chamber, joined from time to time by the others. All of a sudden he heard Manny's voice, deep in an echoing vortex, say the words: 'The killer brass team of 1959.' His stomach turned.

As he made for the door, Manny Kemp followed. 'I'll just make sure he's OK,' he said to the others, and for the second time the door swung. Outside the King's Head Manny unexpectedly put his arm round his former colleague. Then a sudden movement, and the trumpet player fell the five steps from door to pavement, rising to his knees to vomit into the gutter. Manny walked down the steps and watched him. Then quite suddenly his head flicked from right to left.

Then he walked off, his footsteps echoing back from the grit on the rainy pavement.

Who is that Lady???

Avotcja

Betty
  Betty
Betty Carter
   That's right!!!!!
That's who the Lady is
Betty is not just any singer
She's a teacher/preacher/sacred Conjure-woman . . .
. . . Afro-American Goddess of voice
Betty Carter is a song on legs!!!!!
Are you hip to her?
She is walking music
Music that dances . . . hypnotizes
She is the kind of music that makes love to you
Or kicks your behind if you be jiving
You dig??

HEY!!!!!
Her name is Betty!!!
This woman does not sing into a mike
Betty Carter eats up microphones by the dozens
Chews 'em up until they're part of her
Betty Carter is not just a singer . . . I said
She eats, drinks & sleeps music
Her voice is a whole reed/rhythm section
A whole orchestra lives inside of her . . .
. . . Grows stronger every second, every year, with every note
Making us stronger if we be strong enough to listen
Her strength is in refusing to water down the truth . . .
   . . . for an extra nickel or dime

B Flat, Bebop, Scat

Her beautiful double-edged soul . . .
   . . . was created-born B flat/bebop/scat
And it just ain't for sale . . . Jim!!!!!

Betty Carter is her name
And her music is no game
Her powerful powers come from making us powerful
Like the music/woman is strong & gentle . . . And
Like strongly gentle & gently strong . . . strong . . . STRONG!!!
That's right!
That's who the Lady is
Betty is not just a singer . . .
Betty Carter is a song on legs
Are you hip to her?????
   This overpowering
      Always flowering
         Microphone-eating
           Walking music machine

Her name is Betty
   BETTY CARTER . . .
      THAT'S WHO THE LADY IS!!!!!

Faces and Places (For Ornette Coleman)

Anthony Revo

Your hands confirmed that the sun
shone differently on each vertebra.

That your hair abandoned fire for limes
and eucalyptus/that your clothes left the room
speechless/that on Monday afternoon pigeons
fly out of the piano and wings flap in the clouds/
that bricks melt in the sun and tall trees tell
short stories to my feet beneath the ground/that
the leaves have fallen from their dew and walking
the barefoot air I cross the road on a zebra.

That a man can be drunk by his wine and at midnight
on the otherside of the wall a gazelle treads lightly
on a woman's shoes/that a feather fell when you passed
this way. . .

As a bird opened the air you flew into it.

A little Portuguese glass and a peony
beyond the mountains unhinged the swan's neck.

Gone in the Air

Ed Neiderhiser

Born in 1947, Edward A. Neiderhiser is an ordained pastor of the Lutheran Church serving congregations in Philadelphia, PA, USA. Holding a PhD in Old Testament studies, he is published in several technical and ecclesiastical journals. In addition, he is a practising semi-professional jazz performer and composer.

> When you hear music,
> After it's over,
> It's gone in the air;
> You can never capture it again.

Eric Dolphy said that.

Eric Dolphy is dead now. He is over and gone, and you can never capture him again any more than you can his music.

I've read a lot of books about music – music history, music theory, music mechanics, the physics of music, the psychology of music, the psychology of musicians. My library boasts half a dozen shelves of such volumes. After they're read it's over, it's gone in the reading, and nothing of music has been captured. Naught has been captured because the music itself is gone in the air and no part whatsoever of its essence translates to paper.

This is about music, sort of. Whatever it's about, it doesn't translate to paper either. Readers are advised to proceed at the risk of their own confusion. That is the spirit in which the writer continues.

It has been nearly a dozen years since I first discovered one could become the music. No, that's not quite right. One does not become the music.

A reviewer once said about Miles Davis that his performance 'transcends the properties of the horn and becomes the man himself in musical form'. I have always been intrigued by the concept although the name of the particular writer escapes my memory. To become the music, or whatever is quite the right way to say it, is far more than what this reviewer intended in his cute and pseudo-mystical turn of phrase. What I discovered is quite beyond this. Indeed it is so far outside the time–space continuum in which we believe we live as to be virtually indefinable in the language of that time–space frame.

Are we truly bound to the time–space network we call reality? Or are we so locked in by the way we are taught to perceive and respond that we no longer can see alternatives? Is the imaginative world of a child truly imagination? Or is it an alternate dimension that we close off by being raised to conform to the acceptable reality of 'life as we know it'? Is Peter Pan the extension of an imaginative wish by which we can escape into ourselves for a brief moment? Or is it the reflection of a faint residual memory of reality beyond us, once known and left behind? But I stray philosophically; let the story speak for itself.

From my earliest memory, music of all sorts has been a vital and necessary part of my existence. As a child I spent hours enthralled before the speaker of a vintage Philco radio. As a youth I forsook the daily baseball games of my peers to perch hungrily by the ancient RCA turntable that graced the living-room of my home. As a young adult my own array of sound-reproduction equipment and 'stacks of wax', as they say, claimed priority in my attention. From the first stroke of consciousness in the morning to its final fading moments at night I enveloped myself in the nurturing bosom of sound. I accompanied whatever activity was required of me with whatever strains were available. And when none was readily at hand, the memory of what had once passed through the air to my consciousness replayed in my head.

My discovery, or rediscovery, of a reality long ago closed off came about in this way.

It was in my mid-twenties. The entity who, in the usually accepted reality, was my wife at that time was busy with certain personal chores. Her acceptable reality was more narrow than the average, being defined primarily by the most concrete of touchable, handleable, spendable, acquirable stuff. She is no longer my wife in any reality. Our worlds became too divergent. I don't know whose became too rigid to accommodate the other; it doesn't really matter. Simply, whatever we were was gone in the air never to be captured again. Neither of us grieved much.

As she busied herself with her reality late that evening, I sat listening. It was Miles Davis on the stereo, perhaps the Carnegie Hall album, I don't precisely recall. I focused on the sound of the music, the flow of the horn, the interplay of the rhythm, the movement of the harmony. I laid my head back and closed my eyes and suddenly I was in the music, or perhaps on the music, or perhaps. . . Damn! how narrowly language restricts us.

I was outside the body; I was afloat where I had never been before, buoyed by the substance of the trumpet line. I was in essence part of the music; my reality and its were intimately intertwined. I was neither dozing nor hallucinating; I've done both enough to know the difference. I was not, as music-lovers are wont to say, borne up emotionally by the inspiration of the moment or the beauty of the performance. Simply, I was in the air with the sound. I was in, on, integrated with the music itself. I was in a different zone of reality. I was. . .?

There is an old story about a computer that was designed to translate from English to Russian and from Russian to English. Such a device, scientists promised, would remove all misunderstandings from international diplomacy and allow those from opposite sides of the earth to communicate in an uncluttered, unimpaired fashion. (Scientists have perhaps the most narrow of all perceptions of reality.) Into this saviour-computer was entered the common phrase 'out of sight, out of mind'. With appropriate whirring and blinking this epitome of scientific achievement rendered a presumably suitable Russian equivalent. This was then itself re-entered for retranslation into English. The print-out read: 'blind, insane'.

No matter how I try to explain to you what I experienced that night, no matter what words I write, you will most likely read 'blind, insane'. By then I will be gone in the air anyway, so it doesn't matter much. But if a few of you are able to push against the walls of your reality a little, if there are small chinks through which you have momentarily glimpsed the expanse of alternatives, if there are those who clap for Tinker Bell out of genuine belief, perhaps you may perceive a reasonable translation of this inadequate treatise.

I shan't bore you with a detailed rehearsal of the repetitions of the experience. Puzzling and sporadic at first, they later came more frequently and clearly. This time it might be Bach, that time Duke Ellington, perhaps Tchaikovsky, maybe the Rolling Stones. At first it would be only for a moment, a few bars as it were. Then maybe a whole chorus, then an entire performance. Little by little the self-imposed walls of the standard time–space reality were surmounted. Breaches appeared, as voyages of discovery were made into a sphere of reality where none of the laws of the scientists applies. There was only the flow of the music, the reality of melding with the essence of the sound, the existence not of man in musical form but of music as the primary atmosphere.

The second great creed of the Christian faith states: 'I believe in one

God, the Father Almighty, Maker of heaven and earth, and of all things visible and invisible.' Perhaps the greatest of all the heresies of humanity has been to define rigidly the visible and remove all acknowledgement of or participation in the invisible. We have chopped up this God's creation by blocking ourselves in to our own definition of reality and cutting ourselves off from so much of his.

I found that it was possible to enter an alternate state of reality. Not an altered state, for it was never a matter of altering anything. It was always to participate in a dimension beyond the feeble and heretical limits constructed and enforced by man and his society. I've never claimed to be a mystic; indeed I have consciously denied it. Yet I found aspects of the creation in which one could journey that did not conform to the scientific norm that demands the allegiance of 'civilized' man.

The more adept I became at vaulting the wall between the dimensions of reality and taking flight with the music of the moment, the more I realized how artificial the wall was. The reality I was learning to experience was not a separate sphere, but an integral part of the whole of created order. The various dimensions I witnessed and in which I moved were not diametrically opposed to each other but were part of the whole fabric, fabric that had been rent and cut into pieces by the human construction of barriers limiting and stifling the experience of what is real.

There was one unsettling aspect to my journey. I needed a vehicle. The walls by which I was confined were too deeply rooted and too strongly reinforced by years of tacit acceptance. I needed the presence in the air of the music, and I was limited to the vehicles available from outside myself. I could ride them, flow with them, but I could not steer, as it were. I could not determine my own direction through the warp and woof of this dimension. And most disturbing of all, when the performance ended and was gone in the air, I was left back in the reality that bound me by long habit and worldly construction.

I have long been a practising musician as well as a listener, not a great one by any human standards of technical achievement, but good enough to partake of the joys of public performance with some regularity. A second stage of discovery occurred in the course of that pursuit.

It was late one night in a nondescript Philadelphia bar with my own sextet that this next evolutionary, or perhaps revolutionary, step took place. As the band surged and cooked with that collective spark that sometimes makes the whole much greater than the sum of its parts, I suddenly found myself skimming the landscape of that world beyond. Dipping and soaring, I was riding the wave of my own performance. I was providing the vehicle, I was steering, I was charting the course. For the first time I was the pilot and not the passenger. I lowered my horn, exhilarated at the vista now before me.

A liberating power had come into my hands. No longer did I need to wait and hitch a ride whenever and from whomever, but I could come and go as I chose.

The frustrations of the walled-in reality of humanity are well known to all. The bad day at the office, the unexpected interruption, the overdue bill, the rejection by the lover, the loneliness and uncertainty and isolation, all are burdensome because of narrow perspective. All are debilitating, even dehumanizing, because the broader scope of reality has been shut off by the construction of boxes into which we lock ourselves.

Seated at my piano, caressing the keys and shaping the sounds, I could integrate myself in the larger scope of reality, the broader perspective. I joined the music in the air and became an intimate partner in the cosmos, not a separate entity fighting its flow. And I could participate in things visible and invisible according to their design, blending my consciousness with that of the creator.

Final liberation, total integration, however, required yet one more discovery. To vibrate with the music in the air and flow with complete freedom in this ethereal dimension would necessitate an abandonment of any artificial vehicle. I could navigate on the performance of my own music, but why did I need the physical instrument to generate the momentum? Could I not enter this flow of reality solely on the basis of the memory? For while music in performance fades in the air at its completion, never to be recaptured in identical form, none the less its essence is held in the memory ever available to be replayed for the inner ear. Moreover, it is in the mind that the essence of music is created. Any performance flows as expression of the inner creativity. Could the music generated in the mind carry one into this experience even without the physical performance? If so, it would mean that participation in the musical state of reality could be self-generated and thus without limit. The performance need never end, for the musical generation would be internal and not limited by another's composition or physical impetus.

Once again it was late at night. In a bed that was unexpectedly solo, my mind skipped about in the random fashion that is the nature of frustration. I mulled over three things: the persistent and painful loneliness, the aforementioned question, and the opening strains of a new composition that had haunted and eluded me for weeks. Suddenly it all faded except the tune, which thrust itself fully formed into my consciousness. As I mentally played and replayed it, refining and polishing its various parts, I found myself far beyond the conventions of human reality. I was sailing in a world I had touched and explored so often. But this time there was no artificial propulsion, only a self-generated momentum.

As I swung through the break strain, resolving a diminished chord and adding a 9th, a startling thought presented itself: I didn't have to go back. In the memory was the music of the ages, the essence of Bach and Palestrina, Duke and Bird, Mozart and Miles. In the mind was the potential to generate new compositions and performances. In the soul was the ability to recapture and experience and re-create all that had gone in the air and to ride perpetually in that sphere of reality that I had first glimpsed so briefly so long ago.

It is late again tonight. I've thought about it at length. I've made the journey often and have, as it were, earned my wings. I've struggled to integrate the broader experience of reality with the boxes in which society has forced me to dwell. For me it is a lost cause.

Man is a social creature, often much to his own chagrin. In spite of his walls he needs his companion. Yet he resists and blocks the intimacy. I've tasted reality in a wider context. It is more than likely even broader still. I can no longer bear being blocked from the intimacy I seek most.

Tonight I will build my own walls. This time I won't come back. Tonight I will lock myself into that other segment of reality.

This, too, will be a denial of the created order and proper humanity. So be it. God forgive me for rending creation in this way. I will surely find it ultimately as confining and lonely and unsatisfactory as is 'normal' society. Such is the result of any cordoning of creation. But they will be my walls, my choice, my sin.

My body, I presume, will be judged dead and accordingly treated. I doubt if there is anyone who will step from his or her cubicle to mourn too deeply. 'Blind, insane' will be the response of most who will merely be momentarily inconvenienced. My essence, however, will be boxed for its duration in the ebb and flow of music in the air. Second to the right, and straight on till morning.

> When you hear music,
> After it's over,
> It's gone in the air;
> You can never capture it again.

The next time you pause truly to listen to a bit of music, perhaps you will feel for a brief moment the warmth and joy of intimate touch. It will be me, gently and invisibly breaching your walls and caressing your soul.

The Yin Thing

David Kennedy

It was teatime up at the temple
They were warming up the ghee;
The fare there was fairly simple
They liked things additive-free.
The head monk said: 'Ain't this the life!'
As he dished out the curd in lumps
But a very weird spice got in the rice
And made those lamas jump!
   Ow! Who gave a chemical boot
   To the contemplative cats in saffron suits?
   Whoever put a spin in their tantric wheel
   Made the whole monastery rock and reel!
   Where did they get that stuff?
   Now they just can't get enough
   A walk in the foothills of Tibet
   Used to be 'bout as high as a monk could get!

The novices were too pepped up for prayer
Something made them jump around
And the old white monks who never cut their hair
Felt obliged to let it down.
Well they all kicked off their sandals
And some threw off their robes
But they couldn't put a handle
To what scorched their frontal lobes!
   (Repeat chorus)

   Boy that scene was complex
   Like the leaves on a Lotus tree

The Yin Thing

They came to Lhasa by charabanc
To get the hang of the swinging yin and yang

So if the one true path's the one for you
Don't abandon your worldly wealth
Just put on a pair of jiving shoes
And find it in yourself.
Then forget about tofu and ginseng
'Cos all you do is pay the price
Remember the yin thing that's the in thing
Is the spice in the monastery rice
Yeah the yin thing that's the in thing
Is the spice in the monastery rice
Om mani padme hum
Om mani padme hum
Om mani padme hum
Ooroooni!

(With apologies to 'Who Put the Benzedrine in Mrs Murphy's
Ovaltine?')

I Could Write a Book

Clive Davis

Clive Davis was born and raised in Bath. After reading Modern Languages at St Catherine's College, Oxford, he worked as a journalist, contributing to West Indian World, Time Out, City Limits *and the* New Statesman. *He is currently with the BBC and lives in West London.*

I DON'T THINK HE KNOWS EXACTLY WHERE HE WANTS TO STEER YOU, BUT HE KINDA THROWS OUT SOMETHING AND YOU WORK IT OUT WITH YOURSELF. HE MIGHT SAY *SEE!* ‑ BUT YOU KNOW DAMN WELL THAT WASN'T WHAT HE WAS TALKING ABOUT, NOT THAT SPECIFIC THING . . .

He leaned back against the bar, trying to find a pocket of fresh air. That was the one thing he didn't like about this club, any club – the smoke. People didn't realize how important it was for him to keep his lungs in good shape, pure and sweet. Miles didn't realize it either, otherwise he wouldn't have been up there with that filter-tip in the corner of his mouth as he stood and watched the pianist take the solo. Scott could forgive him that vice, though. The band was swinging and Miles was wearing a three-hundred-dollar suit, and the club was full. That was all that mattered. Every table with six people frozen around it, drinks getting warm because everyone was too busy listening to the quintet to worry about anything else. Two hundred pairs of eyes followed Miles' hand as it drifted up to his mouth, took the half-finished cigarette and dropped it on the floor. He tucked his mouthpiece against his lips, ready to play out the number. This one sounded like a cross between 'Neo' and 'Freddie

Freeloader'. Scott hadn't heard it before, but he liked it. He liked everything Miles did.

'Another drink, Scott?' The barman, Jack, picked up the empty glass and gave it a shine, as if he'd just washed it. His mind was on the music too.

'OK, vodka this time.'

Jack brought over an almost-empty bottle and drained it into the glass. More than a double measure, though Scott being a regular, he knew he'd only have to pay for a single.

The barman rested on his elbows and gazed across at the tables. 'Some pretty ladies in here tonight.'

'Yeah, I suppose so.' Scott was still following the quintet. Women came second.

Jack carried on regardless. 'One in the corner over there, looks like Marilyn Monroe, 'cept her chest is too big.'

'Maybe it is her. I hear she likes jazz.'

'Naa, like I said, chest is too damn big.'

Scott sipped at his vodka. 'No pleasing some people, is there?'

The barman's reply was cut off by applause for the end of the number. The band moved straight on into the next one – no bows, no announcements – while Miles stepped off the stage, wiping his forehead with a handkerchief. His skin glistened with perspiration, and his saucer eyes shone even wider in the semi-darkness. He made his way past the tables, past the upturned heads following him intently. He took no notice, or pretended not to. That was his style. And the people went for it.

'Dunno how he gets away with it – just walking off like that,' murmured Jack. 'Not a word to anyone, not even an excuse-me.' He kept his voice down because Miles was heading their way.

'Better fix him a drink,' said Jack, moving off to fetch another bottle. Scott took another sip of vodka, let the flavour hang in his throat before swallowing. Miles seemed to be coming straight towards him through the crowd. He paused every now and then to shake hands with acquaintances, until he was only a few feet away. Scott edged sideways to make some space if the man wanted service.

'Hey, man. Yeah, you.'

Was he talking to him? Scott looked round to see who else it could be. No one. The others were talking among themselves, doing their best not to look star-struck.

Miles spoke again. 'You Scott?'

The voice was little more than a whisper. Everyone had heard the story of how he had almost lost it altogether, after a throat operation. The word was, he'd been sitting in his hospital bed, taking things nice and easy like the doctors told him, when some agent comes in, starts trying to rip him off, cut him out of a deal or something. And Miles gets mad and starts shouting at the guy, forgetting that he wasn't supposed to speak for another few days. And that's how he ruined his voice. Or made himself twice as desirable to women, depending on how you wanted to look at it. Whatever, Scott had to strain to make out what he was saying.

'Yeah, I'm Scott.'

'Thought so. Friend told me 'bout you. Said you play good horn.'

He wondered if this was a practical joke. 'Well, I just mess around when I can, sit in, things like that. Nothing too regular.'

Miles took out a packet of Gauloises and lit up. 'Never mind regular. I hear you're good. I got spies, y'know. Gotta know what's happening.' He drew on his cigarette and blew the smoke high over Scott's shoulder. 'I want you to do me a favour.'

'Sure, what is it?' His head was spinning. Was this happening? To him?

'Look, Scott, tell you what it is. I've gotta split, just a half-hour or so. Said I'd meet my girl at the airport. She's flying in from France. Promised I'd pick her up.'

'Well, why can't you go yourself? They won't stop you here.' He was confused. The airport was more than three hours' drive away, there and back. Miles must have known that.

Miles suddenly went sheepish. 'No, man, I gotta stay here. Missed a set last night because of some chick. The guys here'll get me for breach of contract if I step out of line again. All I want is for you to fill in for me. I can tell 'em we've been working on an album and this is a sneak preview. How about that?'

Scott heard his own voice say yes. The man was pleading with him, he couldn't let him down. Who would? And then he felt Miles taking him by the arm towards a fat, surly-looking man in a white suit sitting at a corner table, who listened while Miles whispered something in his ear. He sat thinking hard for a couple of minutes before nodding and leading the two of them back to the stage. The band rounded off their number so that the fat man could step forward to make an announcement. Somehow, Scott couldn't hear it properly. There was a crazy buzzing sound in his ears which drowned out just about everything else. The odd word slipped through – something about studio collaboration, up-and-coming English talent. He looked out into the darkness where the audience was sitting. It was impossible to make out any faces now, just the outlines of bodies arranged in circles, and the glow of lighted cigarettes everywhere. He was straining his eyes out into the gloom when Miles tapped him on the sleeve and passed him a trumpet case. Scott recognized it as his own.

'You left it by the bar. How d'you think you was going to blow without that?' Miles grinned at him, then strode off, giving a little bow to the customers. Scott heard polite clapping, from the audience and the musicians around him too. He didn't recognize any of them; they weren't Davis' regular quintet. That made him feel more at ease. The pianist gave him a smile, counted the beat and went into the next number. A fast blues. Scott half-recognized it. He waited for his chest to stop thumping and his arms to relax. Strangely enough, it all came easily. He was ready to play.

He soon lost track of the time and how many tunes they got through, though it seemed like a lot. His head was still full of the buzzing sound. He could barely hear the rest of the band though what he could make out sounded good, as if they'd always played together. Nothing too exciting, just neat music. After the first number he looked round to exchange a few courtesies with the rest of the band, a smile or whatever, and to check on what they were going to play next. But then he realized it was dark on stage too now. He couldn't see the musicians, only their instruments silhouetted against a spotlight behind the stage.

'What the hell,' he thought. 'Might as well follow whatever they want to do.'

They played another blues, a slow one this time. At the end he bowed in the direction of the applause. His lip was beginning to ache – he'd never played so much up-front before. He was thinking about that when the applause suddenly died away, and he could hear hushed voices. One was saying, over and over again, 'Hey, look at him. What's happened?'

Then Miles emerged from the darkness and stepped back on stage. Scott noticed something on the side of his face. At first he thought it was beads of sweat. It took him a couple of seconds to see that it was blood.

Miles' voice was still cool. 'Man, looks like you did a good job.'

'You're bleeding.' It was a stupid comment, but it came out anyway.

'Yeah, I know.' Miles seemed unconcerned. 'Ran into some cops outside, when I was bringing in my girl.'

'What do you mean?'

'Yeah, I guess you don't know her.' He dug his hands deep into his jacket pockets and sighed. 'Well, see, she's white, and so were the cops. And they had blackjacks, and my head got busted. That's it.'

Scott watched the blood run down the side of his jaw. 'You'd better get that seen to.'

Miles shook his head. 'No, man, it's cool. Ain't the first time it's happened.' He picked up his horn from beside the drum-kit and prepared to start playing again. ' 'Bout time I finished the set. I was listening to you for a while outside on the sidewalk, before the cops came along. Sounded real good.'

'Thanks.' Scott packed his gear away. He noticed for the first time that he was soaked in sweat. It seemed even darker on-stage now. He could barely see Miles standing a few feet away from him. All he could make out was his eyes.

'I dug that last solo,' said Miles.

'Yeah? I been working on that for a long time. Usually do it when I'm playing with my sextet back home. Maybe you can come and see us next time we've got a gig.'

'You bet.' The man seemed genuinely impressed. 'I definitely wanna hear that.'

HOME: A NEW YORK APARTMENT ON THE EAST SIDE, OFF 5TH AND 70TH, AND A HOUSE IN MALIBU. I LIKE CALIFORNIA, IT'S GOOD FOR MY LEGS, THESE OLD BONES. LAST WINTER I HAD A HIP OPERATION.

'I definitely wanna hear that.' Scott woke with the words echoing in his head. He looked round to where the audience had been, but could see only the familiar shapes of his bedroom clothed in early-morning gloom. His watch said ten past seven. He switched on the radio and listened to a woman talking about a burst watermain in Whitechapel, then sank back on his pillow, breathing heavily, perspiration holding him to the sheets. The dream had been so real. With his eyes shut, he tried to work his way back to the club. Who was Jack? He felt as if they'd been good friends. And Miles, he was just the way he'd always imagined. He opened his eyes again, and they settled on the photograph hanging on the wall at the foot of the bed. He'd bought it from a junk shop in Coventry: a portrait of Miles, *circa* 1961, just like in the dream. Miles in concert, crouching, his horn resting on the floor in front of him. He has his eyes shut and his head turned to the left, as if a cold wind is blowing in his face. To the right, Hank Mobley is playing sax. 'All Blues' – it had to be. And Miles is wearing a three-hundred-dollar suit.

Scott was alone in bed. He felt for his wife, only to find that she had already gone – some time ago, because the bed was cold on her side. She always liked to leave for work early. Scott thought it was to avoid having to speak to him. Still, she'd had time to smoke one quick cigarette, her 'pick-me-up'. The smell still hung in the air. Scott jumped from bed to open the window and let in the morning breeze. The sight of his trumpet case lying on the sill took his mind back to the dream. He'd been brilliant then. If only he could remember how the solos went. In real life, he was decent pub standard, no more. But in the dream . . .

'*I definitely wanna hear that.*' He was in the bathroom, brushing his teeth, a couple of hours later, after he'd finally pulled himself out of bed, when the words came back. The toothpaste still in his mouth, he hurried into the living-room, found his new Miles LP – the one he'd bought the day before – and put it on the stereo. Side one, track four. He listened through, waiting for the words, and picked up a magazine left lying open at the reviews page. He carried on brushing his teeth, absentmindedly, and was about to rinse his mouth out on the carpet when he realized he wasn't in the bathroom any more.

WHICH LEAVES 'FREAKY DEAKY', A STARTLINGLY EERIE TONESCAPE REMINIS-
CENT OF *GET UP WITH IT*'S ELLINGTON HOMAGE 'HE LOVED HIM MADLY', MILES'
SPECTRAL SYNTH DRIFTING FORLORNLY AROUND DARRYL JONES' PROWLING
BASS. 'I DEFINITELY WANNA HEAR THAT,' DAVIS RASPS AT THE END OF THE
TAKE. SO DO I.

The music faded away, Miles' voice came up again. Scott smiled to himself – it was just like in the club. He took a pair of scissors and cut the review from the magazine.

'One more for the wall,' he said, lifting the article out carefully and carrying it to the spare room at the top of the house. There was nothing in the room besides piles of discarded toys and old furniture. And, covering the whole length of one wall, a board with scores of newspaper and magazine clippings stuck to it. All about Miles. He had been collecting them for years. Reviews, profiles, learned essays by people who thought they had something to say but never did, and best of all, interviews – words from the man himself. Whenever he had some spare time, or after a bad day at the insurance company, Scott would go to the room, settle down in a worn-out armchair, and read the cuttings at random or just lazily admire them. His wife made the odd sour comment – she wanted him to spend more time with the rest of the family. But he was a good husband, kept the place tidy, didn't come home drunk in the middle of the night, took the children to Epping Forest on Bank Holidays and cleaned the bath after he'd used it. What was a wallful of fading newsprint compared to that? True, she didn't care much for his habit of bringing home his musician friends once a week. On the other hand, they were a quiet bunch. All they seemed to do was take cans of beer to the room and sit quietly, talking and joking. She had put her ear to the keyhole once, and heard Scott explaining how he had found one of the cuttings in a Dutch newspaper, when they went to Amsterdam for their honeymoon. She remembered it well. He had begged the manager of their hotel to write out an English translation for him. Hearing Scott tell his friends all that made her embarrassed, especially when they burst into laughter. But at least she knew what he was up to, knew they weren't leading him into bad habits.

I HAD TO STOP DOING EVERYTHING. EVERYTHING. LISTEN, I WAS SNORTING COKE, RIGHT, HALF AN OUNCE A DAY SOMETIMES. I WENT OUT DRINKING BRANDY AND BEER AROUND THE CLOCK. I'D GET UP AT MIDNIGHT AND GO OUT ALL NIGHT AND HALF THE DAY, SMOKE FOUR PACKS OF CIGARETTES. I WAS USING SLEEPING-PILLS TOO. I WOKE UP ONE DAY AND I COULDN'T MOVE MY RIGHT HAND, COULDN'T STRAIGHTEN IT OUT. CICELY PANICKED.

'What are you going to do with all that then?' his wife had asked him a few days earlier, gesturing to the wall.

'What d'you mean, *do?*' Scott was busy rereading a piece from a 1968 *Melody Maker*, stuck right at the bottom of the board.

'Well, it must be for something.'

This happened every six months or so, when her puzzlement about the spare room turned her irritable. Deep down, she wanted him to turn the place into a nursery for the children.

'It's not for anything,' said Scott, annoyed at the interruption. 'Maybe I'll use them to write a book some day, I don't know.'

'Yes, and maybe it'll make us millionaires.' She sighed. 'I can't see why you make so much fuss over all this.'

'Why don't you come to the concert and find out? Should be some tickets left.'

Scott knew it was pointless asking her. She didn't like music, not the kind he liked anyway. He fell to thinking about the concert. Festival Hall, seven o'clock. He'd been thinking about nothing else all month. His first chance to see Miles in a decade-and-a-half. He'd been unlucky the two previous years. The come-back gig of '82 had passed him by because his firm decided to send him to Singapore for six months to open a new office. In '83 it was his wife's fault. She was pregnant and went into labour on the day itself. He'd had to stay with her at the hospital. There wasn't even time to get his money back by selling the ticket.

This year would be different.

He'd booked himself a seat in the best part of the hall, right in the front row. No need to worry about rushing home from work to change clothes, because he'd taken the day off. He was going to get there early, drink three and a half pints forty minutes before the gig was due to start, and he would be in seventh heaven. Before that, he had the whole day to himself – no worries, no wife.

He ate his breakfast slowly, savouring every little crunch of cereal. The new LP was playing in the background. He liked it, but he knew his friends wouldn't. They parted company with Miles in the seventies when the music was all congas and wide flairs. That was why they weren't going to the Festival Hall with him; they preferred to stick with their memories and their copies of *Kind of Blue*. Their loss, thought Scott, as he poured himself another cup of coffee. He was going to enjoy himself. He would have a good breakfast, read the newspaper and then go to the West End for the rest of the day, check a record shop perhaps and just wander around like a tourist.

It was a fresh, warm morning when he left the house and took the tube down to Leicester Square. He came up into the sunshine smiling, ready to follow wherever his feet wanted to lead him. He strolled about until lunchtime, treated himself to a good steak and a couple of beers, then drifted back on to the streets, heading towards his favourite second-hand music dealer's. The place was just about empty, not like at weekends. It was luxury to be able to stand at the 'D' section and not be jostled or have some idiot peering over his shoulder, waiting for a chance to get at the records. He rummaged through the titles like a dog at a dustbin blown over by the wind.

'Nothing,' he murmured. It was always difficult to find any Miles LP that he didn't already have. There were fifty-two in his collection – that was including the early stuff with Bird. Nothing, compared with some people he'd heard about. Well short of his own target, too.

He moved on to the bargain bins, hoping against hope. Nothing there either. He wandered outside again. There was a department store opposite. Seeing it reminded him that there was something he had to buy. As he went in, he passed an old man selling newspapers by the entrance. All the familiar stories that helped pass the time on the way to work: Belfast car bomb, Beirut – 70 dead, Poland – more arrests. Belfast and Beirut meant nothing to Scott, but Poland set his mind ticking, racing back to the spare room. It was a little game he liked to play, just to test his memory, especially when he had nothing to do in the office. It took him about fifteen seconds before he could whisper the answer to himself. He was a walking index to his own unwritten book.

'Poland. Right-hand corner. Third from top.'

IN THE CORRIDORS OUTSIDE THE HALL BEFORE THE PERFORMANCE, YOUNG ENTREPRENEURS SOLD WESTERN JAZZ RECORDS FOR UP TO 8,000 ZLOTYS APIECE. DAVIS, AND THE SIX OTHER MUSICIANS IN HIS GROUP, WARMED TO THE POLISH CROWD, WHICH GAVE THEM REPEATED STANDING OVATIONS, CHANTED 'WE WANT MILES' AND SANG THE POLISH SONG, 'MAY YOU LIVE 100 YEARS'. THE JAMBOREE OPENED THURSDAY NIGHT AMID REPORTS THAT STATE-RUN RADIO AND TELEVISION HAD BEEN ORDERED BY THE AUTHORITIES TO

B Flat, Bebop, Scat

The girl behind the counter had been watching Scott for a quarter of
an hour. He didn't look the shoplifting type, but then again, who did
nowadays? He'd been trying on just about every pair of sunglasses on
the rack – he must have got through about thirty already. Each time,
he would check himself in the mirror, then put them back on the
stand, a frown on his face. For some reason, he seemed more
interested in the ladies' pairs, the big round ones. She wondered if
he had sensitive eyes or some sort of illness. Whatever, she wanted
to make sure he didn't plant a pair on his nose and then run out of
the store. They'd lost too many like that.

She walked over and stood behind him. Her voice, when she
spoke, made him jump. 'Can I help you, sir?'

He turned to face her, stammering. 'Yes, I . . . I suppose so.' He
pointed to the ladies' glasses. 'Are these the biggest you've got?'

'I think so. Those are for women, really.'

Scott felt himself blushing. 'Oh, I see. Well, I'm looking for a
particular pair. Very big. It's for a special occasion tonight.'

The girl stepped to one side to make sure she could block his exit if
he tried to make a break. 'How big do you want them?'

'Um, very big.' He realized he wasn't explaining himself very well.
The strange glances she kept throwing his way were making him
tongue-tied.

'I'm fairly sure those are the largest in stock.'

The girl was about to call a supervisor – anyone who could handle
strange men – when he started to fumble for something in his jacket
pocket. She flinched, ready to see a knife come flashing out. It was a
relief when only a photograph emerged. He passed it to her, a
photograph from a newspaper of a black man playing a trumpet on a
stage somewhere. She could tell it wasn't a recent shot because of the
clothes he was wearing – a pair of white bell-bottoms and a striped
shirt with a wide, floppy collar, the kind that went out with the
Osmonds. As for his face, that was hidden behind the biggest pair of
sunglasses she'd ever seen, so big that only his mouth was left
uncovered. It was like looking at the head of a giant bluebottle.

'I'm looking for a pair like that, for tonight.'

She eyed him dubiously. Perhaps he was genuine after all. Perhaps
he was going to a fancy-dress party, or maybe he was an actor and
needed the glasses for some special part. All the same, she couldn't
help him.

'Sorry, we don't do those.' She saw his face cloud over with
disappointment. 'Have you tried Selfridges?'

130

He mumbled something and shook his head. The girl handed him back the photograph. He folded it carefully and put it back in his pocket, then made his way towards the exit. She kept an eye on him, but not for too long — there was someone else loitering at the stand now. She hoped it wasn't another actor.

WHAT FUNK AND BLACK ROCK BROUGHT TO MILES' SPECULATIONS ISN'T UNLIKE WHAT CONSIDERATIONS OF GRAVITY BRING INTO SPECULATIONS ABOUT FOUR-DIMENSIONAL SPACE—TIME — NAMELY A FEELING FOR HOW THE EARTHLY PARTS OF OUR BEING IMPACT UPON OUR PERCEPTIONS OF THE COSMOS, SPACIALLY AND TEMPORALLY. AND SIMILARLY TO MODERN PHYSICISTS, MILES FOUND IN EMBARKING UPON HIS ELECTRIC JOURNEY THE RELATIVITY OF HIS QUANTUM EXPERIMENTS TO THE EVERYDAY EBB AND FLOW OF AFRO-AMERICAN POPULAR CULTURE.

Less than an hour to go before the concert, Scott meandered through the walkways outside the hall, happy to lose his way among the concrete slabs. One minute he was sinking into the dank belly of the Hayward Gallery; the next he found himself back on the heights, overlooking the Thames. It wasn't really the place to see jazz — free jazz, maybe, but not the real thing. He whiled away a few minutes watching a busker play tenor on Hungerford Bridge. The wind was playing games with the notes, picking them and tossing them off the bridge in all directions. Scott couldn't concentrate on the music anyway. He felt too nervous, nervous in the stomach, as edgy as he had been all those years ago when he played his first pub gig. And he wasn't even playing tonight, only listening.

The afternoon had passed quickly. Looking for the sunglasses had taken up a lot of the time, though he hadn't found any he liked. Thirsty from all the walking around, he went into the foyer of the hall and bought a soft drink in the bar. He told himself he would have a beer a little later, just as he had planned. There weren't many people about yet, apart from a few commuters enjoying a glass of wine before they slipped off to join the crush across the road at Waterloo. He took his drink and sat in an armchair near a group of youths in leather jackets and jeans — students, he supposed — lounging around a table full of beer glasses, engrossed in a friendly argument. Scott tried to shut it out and think of what lay ahead in the evening. He wondered what Miles was doing. Practising in his dressing-room? Drinking, like him?

A voice cut through his thoughts, a drawl trying to pass itself off as street-level. 'Like, after Coltrane went, that's where he started going downhill. He needs guys who can give him some competition. No, honest, that's what I think. I mean, the music now, it's all right, but it's nothing special. Same with everything he's done since '69.'

Another drawl interrupted. 'No, Pete. That's what a lot of people say, 'cos they haven't given it a chance. You should read this guy's piece in *Downbeat*. He tells you what the modern stuff's all about.'

Scott gulped down his drink and went to fetch the beer he'd promised himself. As he stood waiting to be served, he thought about phoning his wife. He'd told her he would, just to check that everything was all right. As if the house was likely to burn down while he was away. He decided that she could wait; he would ring before catching the tube home. This was his night.

The argument was still winding its way round the table when he sat down again. 'He ought to know what he's talking about, Pete – he did a thesis on Miles for his PhD.'

'So?'

'So, he knows what he's talking about, that's all.'

The other voice let out a sigh. 'Oh, stuff that. I don't care, as long as he hasn't got that guitarist with him tonight.'

'Who's that?'

'You know, the one who looks like Meat Loaf.'

They all laughed at that.

Scott dipped in and out of the conversation while he watched more people arriving through the doors: smart young executives who got the bug with *Bitches Brew* when they were at college; greying men who would tell you that the only way to listen to jazz was on 78s in a corn field; Police fans who wanted to see the man that Sting was always talking about in interviews.

The five-minute bell caught him daydreaming. His first instinct was to jump to his feet, then he relaxed. He knew Miles wouldn't be starting on time – he never did. He sank back into his chair, breathed deeply. It was strange, his nerves had gone, everything was calm once more. It must have been the beer, he thought. It had been like that before the pub gig. He closed his eyes and relaxed. The voices around him faded away.

And then he was walking back on-stage and playing, caught in the spotlight. Only this was no club. He could see thousands of people sitting in the darkness beyond the lights. Tier upon tier, rows of faces ascending as far as he could see, until they were no more than stars on a misty night. All of them listening to his solo. He couldn't hear what kind of sound he was producing – everything was drowned out by the pounding of guitar, bass and drums. He saw that there were stacks of amplifiers on either side of him, producing a roar which reduced his body to nothing but vibrations, running from head to toe like a dull electric shock. He kept playing, improvising to the changes, and glanced across at the other musicians standing about twenty feet away. Two black and one white. In their early twenties, no more. What they were playing seemed to him more like R&B than jazz, but at least it was easy to follow. He could work around a riff, and as long as the audience was happy, there was nothing else he had to do.

There was the sound of an electric piano as well now, running up and down scales. He looked across again and realized there was a bank of keyboards tucked away in the far corner, so high that it completely hid whoever was playing. Scott had his eyes fixed on it when the tempo suddenly dropped. He waited, not sure what he was expected to do, until he saw a figure emerge from behind the keyboards – Miles, playing muted horn, a fragmented melody that had tinges of 'My Funny Valentine'. His head was bowed, the horn pointing straight down to the boards. He carried on blowing as he slowly walked across the stage towards Scott. He was limping a little, but otherwise . . .

Otherwise, he looked just the same as at the club. The same three-hundred-dollar suit. And not a day older. The only thing different was the limp, and the way he was hunched over the horn. The audience was silent, waiting for every note. Women in dark glasses cradled their heads in their hands, frozen in concentration. Others nodded gently in time. Miles crouched low at the front of the stage to let the photographers scramble for their close-ups, before he was up and on his way again towards Scott. He came to the end of the solo just as he reached him, as the women in dark glasses burst into applause. He looked up at Scott for the first time. And then there was that rasping voice.

'Scott, what kept you, man? We been waiting for you. Come on, we gotta send 'em home happy.'

Miles Smiles

David Pepperell

Miles
the black prince
appearing at the blackhawk
                              tonight
in the air
                expectancy hangs
a tinkling of glasses in the negro night
waiters whispering in corners
for Miles
the black prince

A footfall at the door
the doorman raises his cap in salute
there is a burberry over the shoulders
of Miles
the black prince

Miles
walks past the assembled tables
without acknowledgement
to friend or foe
Miles has nowhere to go
                          except ahead
to the back area of the stage
where he holds court not with his peers
for there are no equals
to Miles
the black prince

B Flat, Bebop, Scat

Later he held his golden horn
to his dark lips
and forced the night to unwind
but by that time
just about all that could be said
                              had already been
 for we all had seen
Miles
the black prince

The Blue Bayou

Julio Finn

Julio Finn is a blues musician and writer. He has travelled and performed with Muddy Waters, Howling Wolf, Chicago Beau and Memphis Slim as well as with jazzmen Archie Shepp, Anthony Braxton and the Art Ensemble of Chicago. He has recently finished a study of hoodoo and voodoo in the blues and is currently writing a book about Negritude.

> If you're goin' to de bayou
> — you'd better take a mojo-offerin' with you.
> Hoodoo Slim

Invocation

Praise be unto the Loas
— as 'twas in the days of old!

Praise be unto the Ancestors
— may their true story be told!

We seek permission for this child to enter
— by Your grace — the land of the Hoodoo Man!

Aye, without the Gate he waits
— black gesso for Your divine hands!

B Flat, Bebop, Scat

Forty-odd miles north of New Orleans the bayous take on a particularly forbidding aspect, the foliage becoming so dense that the great swamp is always dark. The sun seems to deny it its light – indeed, such is the gloom of this saturnine swampland that it is enrapt in the mantle of an indescribable loneliness, as of having never suffered human presence. The eerie stillness of its waters, the blinding shadows, the haunted silence – all add up to the terrifying ghastliness of a wild and bewitched wasteland. Nothing here is as it is elsewhere: colours, bathed in the preternatural light, take on hallucinatory hues; the myriad constellations of plants exhale veritable mists of benumbing fragrances. It is the canvas of some demonic artist, a living mural depicting a deadly reality: *the bayous live by incessantly dying*. And it is this perfect defect which magnetizes lonesome travellers, drawing them into it. For once seen by human eyes, the bayous cannot but become a lesson, at once a tableau of the mysteries of life and the key to those mysteries. Once truly experienced, they become a mirror of the soul, its dramas and rites of initiation.

The lords of these almost uninhabited domains are the hoodoo men, the root doctors, men and women so inextricably enmeshed in the lore of the country their ancestors were stolen from that they are unequipped for the way of life of the towns. Theirs is the primitive way of teleology and homeopathy, the worship and pacification of the divine spirits, as practised in age-old African tradition. To these holy herbalists the bayous are both temple and medicine chest; natural sanctuaries where they can live out their lives according to the dictates of their faith. Here there are no preachers to tell them to believe in the White God, no policemen to harass them for being charlatans. In this lost corner the hoodoos are free to cultivate that harmony which is a balance between interior and exterior forces. Their existence is at once preposterously simple and incredibly complicated: nothing is either impossible or taken for granted. The bush doctors' worldview is a maze of interdependencies, of symbols and metaphors, signs and interpretations, rewards and sacrifices. They are at once hierophant and acolyte, and are rulers of Nature only so long as they are rulers of themselves. They are the evangelists of a persecuted religion in a hostile land; apostles of outlawed rites smuggled into the New World. Because of their special connection with the gods, people came to them for their miraculous powers, for *wangas* and *mojos*, magic charms which would ensure good fortune and protect them from evil: fix-it powder; get-rich lotion; black-cat bone; unbeatable gambler's *wanga*; lover's cure-all – and scores of other never-fail talismans. While willing to profit from these rustic sages' divinely inspired knowledge, the people mistrusted them, and usually gave the swamps they lived in a wide berth. Thus, ignorance and legend had made certain bayous no man's lands. Publicly, people might put hoodoo down as 'hooey', but no one was willing to put the rumours of unholy ceremonies to the test. And so to common belief the bayous remained the abodes of malignant spirits and conjurors, or voodoo *mambos* and fetishers.

Some time early on in this century a man with a guitar slung across his back entered the hamlet of La Rouge at dusk. The people treated him with what would in any other place be described as xenophobia, but is known in these outlands as minding one's own business. Besides, he had all the suspicious hallmarks of the drifter, which among these cautious folks amounted to a licence for immorality. But it was the guitar which put him beyond the pale and relegated him to the level of a hobo. A bluesman! Everyone knew what that meant: he was a singer of the devil's music, songs unfit for Christian ears! Unable to attain lodging for the night, the hobo lay down under a tree, his sleep watched over by two of the more vigilant members of the community. Next morning he crossed the creek and branched off into the swamp, for what ungodly reason the people of La Rouge could scarcely guess – not unless he was going to seek out Papa Gil, the hoodoo man. It had been a long time since anyone had done that, way back when that feller had come up from New Orleans seeking the spirit of Queen Marie Laveau, and had had to be carried out of there half out of his mind. Since then, no one had penetrated the Papa's swamp, that sullage of infamous memory. As for Papa Gil himself, the things related about him were uniformly frightening. He was said to be the oldest person in the bayous – at least 120 years old; he stalked the bogs in a huge black cape and hat, and was attended by cats and bats; he sacrificed to the Lord of Darkness by the light of the full moon; and, among other unwholesome gifts, he had the power to transport himself hundreds of miles in a split second. Hence his incredible control over his territory, over which he watched with a jealous eye.

The deeper the hobo penetrated into the marsh, the more cautious he became; every step took him deeper into that daytime night, full of unknowns. He walked like a man with a mission – steadily but stealthfully. Whatever it was he wanted, he wanted it badly, for even the sense of escapeless peril didn't make him turn back. He was afraid of the novelty of his situation, of plunging into a world in which he himself was his sole succour in event of disaster. According to legend, all kinds of creatures – earthly and unearthly – lurked in the swamps, and this one in particular had the reputation of being peopled by duppies and hobgoblins. Contending against these fears, the heat and the unpredictable, slimy road under his feet, he trudged on, kindling his courage with the thought of achieving his quest.

A gentle movement in the air told him that the sun was cooling down and, sure enough, when he arrived at the next clearing, the sky was a diaphanous blue, as serene as crystal. The foliage, reflected helter-skelter on the water, stretched away to the horizon like a verdurous sea. Imperceptibly, his fear changed to awe and, like a man bewitched, he strode forward into the unfolding black blossom of the night.

Once arrived within sight of the abode of the hoodoo doctor he sat down, more to clear his thoughts than to rest his body. Instinctively, his guitar found its way into his hands, and at once his fingers released clusters of soft, blue notes into the evening air. Unconsciously, he gave himself up to beguiling fantasies, in the train of which came memories of his recent past: the gang which congregated around the bandstand at Jake's; Lou-della whispering thrills into his ear; the dancers caught up in their fiery tribute to rhythm. Then the whole of the Black Bottom, the black people's part of town, rose before him – vibrant and searing in its struggle for life. He saw his grandmother – one among countless other grandmothers – going to work as a house-cleaner in the white neighbourhood. He saw his father and mother – lost in the infinity of other fathers and mothers – working in the fields, sweating their lives away for wages too low to sustain that thankless existence. He saw the juke joints under the spell of the gods of booze, frustration and frenzy – and understood that, even in this, there was a kind of logic . . . and the notes began to fly from his guitar like sparks, like thoughts so sanguine that they could be expressed with safety only in an isolated place.

The hoodoo man's shanty seemed undecided as to whether it should stand or collapse. Through the open door the traveller could see that it resembled nothing so much as a botanical warehouse – gourds, satchels and plants made up the bulk of its furnishings. Then, before he could announce himself, he heard someone stir and, slowly, like an image taking shape on a developing photographic print, a silhouette formed in the doorway. An old man, clad not so much in clothes as in beads and bracelets, stood there. His face struck the hobo as something wondrous and rare, and his eyes seemed to reflect the fire of stars. His face expressing the fear and awe he felt, the hobo attempted to speak but couldn't, attempted to raise his hand but couldn't do that either. The silence which bonded them was a hieroglyph of the void which separated them.

Sitting at the crossroads in the middle of the night, the man with the guitar replayed in his mind what had transpired between himself and the hoodoo man. Having finally found his tongue, he explained that he had sought him out because he wanted to make a pact with the devil, so that he would have power over music. Having heard that he, Papa Gil, was the greatest of the hoodoos, he had come to him, in the hope that he would use his magic to assist him in attaining his end. To all this the old man had listened with inscrutable indifference. After a pause, he had condescended to ask the supplicant only one question, almost baffling in its simplicity.

'How did you get here?'

Whatever store he put by its answer, he must have been satisfied, for he went into his shack and returned with a charm which he gave to the man. 'Take that,' he told him, 'down to the crossroads, and offer it to the devil – I can guarantee the result.' Then, having directed him to the nearest conjunction of the roads, he unceremoniously retired.

And now the man was squatting there, his guitar on his lap, waiting for the devil to appear. Though trembling with fear, he never doubted his ability to see the thing through – even though the price to be paid was his soul, he was ready to sacrifice it in order to become a Faust of the blues. Indeed, his love of the music was such that he felt his soul a small thing to lose if the quality of his music could redeem his life. Now, let the devil come and put him to the test!

Dreamlike, enrapt in the mysterious aura of the bayous, with each instant seemingly a moment of truth, he sat and waited, expecting the devil to rise out of the drifting mists and take shape. Several times he could have sworn that he heard footsteps, and once even a voice – as if someone was calling his name. But the hoodoo man had warned him about leaving the place where he had offered the charm, and so he stuck to his post. Anyway, if it was the devil calling, he knew where he could find him. Then, as dawn broke, he was forced to admit that he had wasted his time, that the sacred hour had passed.

Possessed with rage, he stood before the old man's hut, shouting abuse – 'Old fake, damned impostor, shyster, hoodoo hooligan!' He had a good mind to give the rapscallion a lesson with his fists, to see that living ghoul on to that nether heaven beloved of his ilk. Then, with pitying sarcasm, he came out with what he had known all along – namely, that all that talk about hoodoo was simply a lot of bunk, old wives' tales used as mumbo-jumbo to frighten children.

'I told you true,' the hoodoo man retorted, 'when I said that I could guarantee the result of your useless and vain sacrifice, and things have turned out just as I predicted. You came here overloaded with ignorance – about yourself, me and the power you sought – yes, puffed up and seeking supernatural strength. Fool, you know neither that which you seek nor whom you seek it from. You called the Lord of the Crossroads the "devil" – and after that blasphemy you expect him to fulfil your silly wishes! And I'll bet you don't even know why you think of him as the devil. It's because you believe in the white man's god – well, then, ask *him* to grant you your wish! It's clear to see that you've put your hopes of salvation in the whites . . . when I asked you how you'd got here, you told me that you'd walked! Idiot! Don't you know you were brought here on a slave ship? Don't you know that you were auctioned like cattle, then fattened like a pig so as to fetch a high price? Haven't you the sense to see that the white man used his god to gain a hold over your will? No, you have seen nothing, realized nothing – and thus you will suffer under the white man's yoke till your dying day!'

This diatribe hit its recipient like an illumination. So irresistible were these truths that he could only retreat before them. The implications were dire: he was the offspring of slaves who, for some unfathomable reason, had sought to forget that fact. But how could he when, as was now clear, it was the determining factor in his destiny! Even his music was the product of it, and to forget slavery was to destroy his music's relevance. Black people, blues music: the two were interchangeable, blood relations, affiliated by suffering. The corollary was that to be black was to be blue; the music was the black people's shadow. The old man's wisdom had revealed this to him, and he was determined to tap the source of that wisdom.

'First,' the hoodoo man admonished him, 'you must be initiated into African worship, the worship of the ancestors. We slaves were brought from Africa, so our true gods are those of that place. We hoodoo men are practitioners of African science and African rituals – we believe in our ancestors. With their help you can become a man of power; without them, you are nothing. Know, then, that the *loas*, the gods of your people, are eternal spirits who dwell within you – you must learn to recognize them and to heed their commands. And woe to him who ignores them! For they are jealous spirits, and demand worship. You must put aside the white man's Jesus, under whom you are reduced to a pawn. Without the least knowledge of these things you wanted to make a pact at the crossroads – know, son, that to acquire the power of a *loa* one must first become possessed, and you must be trained to handle possession. Had the Master of the Crossroads possessed you that night, you would have

spent the rest of your life as a lunatic wandering through the bayous!
I can see from your face that the idea of being possessed scares you,
but you need have no worry about that. Contrary to what people
think, to be possessed by a *loa* is a sign of merit, for they will only
"mount" those who are worthy. This is part of your birthright. So,
give up these unmanly fears – in order to receive the power of the
loas you must prove yourself a man of power. To succeed at the
crossroads you must have knowledge as well as faith.'

Matter-of-factly, the hoodoo man also spoke to him about music.
According to him, music was also a form of power, a rhythmic way
of praising the ancestors and binding the people. He remembered the
great voodoo meetings held on the bayous during the reign of Marie
Laveau, the Hoodoo Queen of New Orleans, when hundreds of the
faithful had congregated to praise the ancestors with dance, song and
music; nights seemingly without end, when the Arada drummers
had lured Damballah and Erzulie into their midst; when Baron
Samedi had appeared, brandishing his great sword; when Papa
Legba, the Keeper of the Gate and Master of the Crossroads, had
personally escorted the queen through the swamps. In those happy
times the bayous rang with the jubilation of a thousand voices, and
the thunder was drowned by the booming syncopation of a hundred
drums.

It was nearly midnight when he reached the place where the two
narrow roads met. The bayous, pungent with smells, were a
cacophony of spooky sounds. He had been consumed by fear, but
now he was determined to go through with it, excited by the idea of
leading a more authentic existence. Henceforth, he would be
different from other men, gloriously damned! The bluest man in the
Delta! With the moon as his witness, he began to follow the old
man's instructions. First he saluted the Four Quarters, and then
sprinkled the voodoo dust on the ground in the form of a circle. Next
he put the John the Conqueroo *wanga* around his neck and squatted
at the meeting of the crossroads, with his guitar on his lap. Then,
closing his eyes, he invoked Legba, using the secret words the
hoodoo man had revealed to him. And slowly, the words began to
take effect – he felt his mind loosening, being freed from its normal
trammels. He became aware of the world in a way in which he had
never experienced it before: the whole bayou seemed to be adhering
to some omnipotent, universal force – its foliage, its creatures, its
waters – all seemed to be calling his name. Branches reached out to
touch him; the ground rose and fell under him; the air became a
cornucopia of voices – caressing, promising, mocking, cursing

voices; cries, wails, howls. Now, there could no longer be any doubt; he was being possessed! Antibon Legba was coming to him, coming to 'open the gate'! Then came the faces – frightful contortions, abominable combinations of human and animal features whirling bodiless through the air. Simultaneously he desired to escape, was fleeing, was pinned to the earth; he had never come here, he had fled, he would be there for ever. He was beyond time, with time, Time itself. A slave ship, vaster than the whole of the bayous, came towards him, coasting on a sea of tears. One great, insufferable lament arose from within its bows, and then went echoing through eternity. Tens of millions of black women came to him, holding out to him their babes, whom they had saved from slavery by taking their lives. Of a sudden distant rumbles were heard approaching from the Four Quarters, and he prepared himself for the coming of the great god himself. But as he was looking into the distance, he suddenly became aware that the *loa* had snuck up on him from within – Legba the Trickster! A hurricane of drums swept through him – and he realized that he himself was both the drummer and the drum. His hands and feet were whirling in every direction, using the air for a tom-tom. Then the beat broke out within him, knocking him about in the air, bouncing him along the ground. A multitude of hands hammered away inside him. Papa Legba celebrated his coming with a divine tattoo until, finally, satiated with joy, he laid his devotee down, Rhythm reborn in the form of Man.

To John Ehle

Drum Solo

Sue May

This is the rain
This is the rain
This is the rain rain rain
Rain falling rain falling
Falling rain on the fallen leaves
This is the distant
Faraway train
This is the thunderstorm
This is the rain
A snake in the spotlight
Speaking yes
Sudden, of a sudden
Pistol shot
Heart beating time
Road running
This is a cat being stroked to sleep
You in a warm coat
This is a paintbrush playing sandpaper
A snake hissing
A piece missing
Or maybe the falling petals kissing
Is a bad man kicking cans
Is it you coquettish, behind a fan
Or a bangerbangerbanger bang
Cars on the wet road
Say to the night I wish I wish
I wish I wish

Saint Leroy

Avotcja

Leroy Brooks killed himself a year ago
All alone, in a garage, with nothing but his drum sticks
And maybe his sock-cymbal & brushes
He wrote a short note, and the gas painlessly did him in
But the whole world murdered him
   While they drank a little more wine
     While they built another bomb
       While they trained another 'ass-tronaut'

My friend Leroy died a year ago . . . a whole year ago
And they told me about it just this afternoon
Three hundred days too late to hold his hand
Not soon enough to dry his tears
Too late to say, 'Please don't Baby!
   . . . You can't do it!!'
Too God-damned late!!!

Leroy, everybody's brother, the drummer's drummer, and no one's
   lover
You know, he used to straddle his drums
Better than most men do their women's thighs
Did it help to kill him because he never straddled mine
You know he killed himself last year
   All alone
     With nothing but his drum sticks

Gentle Leroy, always the musician, never a person
Too sensitive . . . Too much a human being

148

A real live human MAN in a world of machines that never cry, or
   hear
A Prince, in a world where geniuses are lepers (or mad men)
This ugly, cold world destroyed him, castrated him,
   . . . killed him, MURDERED HIM!
And all the new, up-coming, young musical cannibals
. . . chewed on the bones of his rhythms
And everybody sings his praises now that he can't hear them

But Spirit-land must be a wee taste better than this living hell
They've got all our best
   Billie Holiday/Eric Dolphy
     Charlie Parker/Memphis Minnie
      Bessie Smith/John Coltrane
       Booker Little/Dinah Washington
And most of all they've got Leroy Brooks
   Maybe now he has someone to talk to
     To hold hands with
      To look at life with

My friend Leroy killed himself last year
A little too soon to tell him how much I loved him
A long time too late to tell him that I miss him
Or is it?
   LEROY?? ? ?? ??

Blevins' Blues

Elaine Cohen

A New Yorker, Elaine Cohen read Anthropology at the University of Chicago, where in 1971 she was awarded the Academy of American Poets Prize, the Menn Foundation Award for Fiction, and was exposed to the blues and avant-garde jazz of the Southside. During the 1970s she wrote, travelled extensively and performed poetry with musicians and dancers. She is the San Francisco correspondent for Coda, *and has contributed to* Downbeat, Cadence, Swing Journal *and* Jazz World *in addition to publishing a ten-year collection of poetry,* Closer to the Source, *in 1979. In 1985 she completed a biography,* Unfinished Dream, *written in collaboration with its subject, Red Callender.*

J.A. Blevins dozed on the bed until a scant knocking woke him. He jumped up, opened the door. The corridor of the Wabash Arms Hotel was empty, silent.

Instead of lying down again, he went to the sink and splashed his neck and arms with water. The mirrored face stared back at him. He saw a strong, proud, fiery man approaching fifty. The white patch running diagonally through his dark beard betrayed his youthful brow. Despite the reddened edges, there was a curious radiance in his eyes tonight, a glow he hadn't seen in quite some time.

Hungry, he surveyed the rickety table that served as kitchen in his cramped room. A fat cockroach marched defiantly across the mustard jar.

'Die!' he commanded, flicking the roach away. Then he noticed unmistakable evidence between the hot sauce and the celery salt.

Quickly, he stepped to the sink, scrubbed his hands. In the mirror now he saw a disgusted frown. The mouth twisted downwards, hideously distorted, the eyes narrowed to bulging slits. Repelled by this Hyde-like vision, he went back to bed and lit a cigarette.

Again he heard that faint knocking sound.

'Cool it,' he whispered harshly.

The scratchy knocking stopped. Silence in the room, a silence made possible by noises from the street. Again that scratch. He knew he was not alone. A mouse was nothing to J.A., but this evening he desired solitude so ardently that he shouted in fury: 'Mouse! I know you're here! You left your slime on my kitchen table. Now you know I know.'

He got up and paced the room with emphatic footsteps. Angrily, he smacked the radiator with a shoe. True restful solitude was now impossible. Musing on this foul but predictable turn of events, he sat down.

'I could rot up here in this lousy firetrap, and nobody give a damn. You know who I am, you little squeak-box? Know who you're messing with? One of the greats, baby. One of the Ones. You dig?

'What the hell do you know? You just a mouse. You ain't payin' no rent. Least you could do is say "yeah". Say "yeah" mouse.'

The mouse crept from its hiding-place under the bureau on to the frayed carpet. It stood on its hind legs for a second as if to say 'YEAH' then crumpled to its usual four-pawed position, ready to scamper back to the wallboard. Throughout these mouselike motions, it maintained a dignified air, a certain exact stubbornness not unlike J.A., who laughed loudly for several minutes until he heard banging on a nearby wall.

'Don't go away,' he told the mouse. 'Don't move,' he warned, adjusting his stingy-brim hat in the mirror.

The mouse retreated to a shadowy corner. With a backward glance, J.A. pulled the door shut and retreated down the dingy stairs past the desk clerk, on to the street to the liquor store conveniently located two doors from the hotel.

The bottles were displayed under glaring fluorescent lights: Gallo Thunderbird, Ripple, Mad Dog 20-20, White Port, Tokay, Muscatel, etc. Scorning all sweet, even drier varieties of burgundy and chablis, he inched his way through these inferior beverages to that certain tall dark green bottle. Distinctively shaped, with silver-and-white label, it contained the ingredient he craved: dry vermouth.

He seized the cheapest kind. For him the cheapest had merits that the most rare expensive wines held for vintage connoisseurs. J.A. Blevins was indeed a gourmet in this category, having sampled them all in his time. Paying his $1.79, he hastily marched back to confront the mouse.

The room was as he'd left it, but the mouse was not visible. He sat down on the bed, opened the bottle and took a long swig. The vermouth had a bitter, oily consistency, not unlike turpentine. He wiped his mouth on his jacket sleeve and exhaled gratefully. The potent liquid began its descent. From throat to fingertips it travelled through him, down his spine, signalling the familiar 'on' sensation.

Now he had no qualms about going to the befouled table. Meticulously he rinsed a glass and filled it to the brim with that pale-yellow necessity. Almost at once his glass was drained. Again he felt that welcome surge. A slight sweat beaded his upper lip. He smiled.

'Mouse!' he called out, 'show yourself, you weakling. I know you're here. Hide all you want, but you stand revealed!'

He glimpsed the mouse scurrying from under the bed to the table.

'All right. That's better.'

Taking short sips of the vermouth, his mind drifted into the past . . . he was up on the bandstand . . . 2,3,4, his fingers popped.

'Ever heard'a Louis Armstrong, mouse? Fats Navarro? Those cats'll kill you, man. Ever heard'a Charles Yardbird Parker? You – hey you – I'm talking to you. Shit, you better listen . . . get out from under my table, mouse!'

Slowly, cautiously, the mouse advanced a few steps.

'Yeah. OK.' More sips of wine and the desired effect was coming through. Wine in his bloodstream produced that ever vital intensity. It transformed his aura, let him breathe easier. Power seethed through him. He stood up, hooked his fingers around the invisible valves of his battered, absent trumpet. Shoulder scrunched, his feet fell into an accustomed stance, the only possible stance. His thirty years playing trumpet had perfected this position.

'De De De, De De De, De De De – DAAAAAA' . . . Holding the last note, he nodded to the invisible bass player.

Out from under the table, the mouse stood on its haunches. J.A. looked down at it, kept tapping his foot. At a precise moment, he pointed to the drummer and the saxophonist, held one beat and stepped back in preparation for his solo. Apparently the mouse heard something too. It stood quietly relaxed. Whether or not it heard the exact high-energy sounds that were racing and spiralling through J.A.'s mind was unclear.

'Hey mouse – we played this one in Paris.' Keeping time with his foot, he listened with great attention to this concert the wine had activated.

The mouse moved forward with a dancing sway, head bobbing from side to side. It looked up at J.A. whose eyes were closed, whose body was poised as if for flight. At the cymbal break the soloist reassumed his stance, ready to join the saxophone player for the bridge.

Then would come his most potent solo, a delight and harsh surprise to the expectant audience: Europeans, some American GIs and naturally, the press. All he heard was the first note. This note contained the seeds for the yet unknown and perfect notes to follow. Opening his eyes he saw the mouse at his feet in a frenzied sway, circling round and round. The sight of this two-inch creature in dervish throes threw J.A. into a rage.

'*Faggot!*' he screamed and cast the imaginary trumpet down. Shocked, the mouse halted. After a momentary retreat, it began circling J.A. with neat, dainty steps.

'*Faggot!*' he shouted again. The mouse paused, then backed slowly to the bureau, fear rippling its back and neck, beady-eyed, tremulous. Paralysed with dread, the mouse froze. There was evil intent in J.A.'s eyes despite himself, for he had no conscious desire to destroy the mouse. Yet, the trembling, cringing creature on the floor – weak, helpless – drove him berserk.

He grabbed the mouse by the tail and ran to the window, needing to hurl it from his presence. The window was stuck. One last shred of control remained. If he smashed the window he might damage his playing hand, his musical knuckles. It was too great a risk; he had to maintain their supreme flexibility.

So he turned to the opposite wall. The mouse wriggled, squeaked, dangled by its tail.

He snarled in disgust at its frailty, hurriedly moving to the door. In his haste he banged his knee on the iron bedstead. Even this sharp pain could not deter him. 'Later for you, rodent,' he shouted as he opened the door and flung the mouse into the hallway.

Bewildered, the mouse landed on its back, righted itself and stared deep into J.A.'s eyes before scurrying down the sunless passage.

J.A. slammed the door. He poured another drink, tossed it off, while gratefully regarding his unmarred knuckles. Another glassful and all he had left was a swallow.

For a long time he sat on the bed, the empty glass in hand. Dusk, with its luminous shadows, crept in at the window. Finally he got up and went to the mirror. The face staring back at him was somehow different.

'Do you know who I am?' he asked the face. A loud guffaw echoed through the room. He put on his jacket, adjusted his hat, searching in the shadows for cigarettes. These found, he put them in his jacket, but not before downing the corner of wine left in the bottle.

'Time for another round,' he said. 'Let's go see if what I need is out there tonight.'

A hard wind slapped him on the cheek. The streets were littered with junkies, empty beer cans. Glittering shards carpeted the alley. He drifted through it. The wind suddenly changed direction, became tender.

He hailed a cab and mumbled directions. They drove for miles. When J.A. looked out the window at an unfamiliar neighbourhood he told the driver to stop; handed him the fare and got out. The cab roared away.

'Damn, where is everybody?' J.A. said aloud as he surveyed the bleak location. Dusk piled in around him. He began to walk towards the setting sun. Three dogs appeared, trotted rapidly past him, then disappeared into shadows. An unseen hand flicked a switch. Rows of streetlights flashed on, beading a network that converged on the horizon.

Through railroad yards, past factories, housing projects. His feet began to hurt. He crossed the expressway and continued east, towards Lake Michigan. A train whistle made him stop, listen.

He shuddered. A melody flooded him, an entire composition. 'I'll call it "The Bullfight". Nothing standard . . . the "Alchemical Bullfight",' thought J.A. . . . As usual, the bull paws the ground. The matador flings his red cape. The picadors are ready yeah, the picadors, a fleet of flutes. The crowd is tensed.

The reeds swell, the trombones sigh, a trumpet signals. The bull changes direction like a bird in flight.

So far it's a classic, he thought . . . The bull is beginning to sweat. The stench rises in the matador's nostrils, the bull charges. Four tubas take over in low spurting jabs. Underneath, congas and the bass drum tango. All holds: the standoff duet – two tenors, the flaring red cape. The bull paws the ground and regroups.

Oh, this music! . . . Suddenly the bull circles the matador-trumpet, cymbals glint in the afternoon sun, the trumpet hits altissimo G.

Silence. Then the picador-flutes revive. A triangle is sounded. This clear bell-like tone unnerves the crowd. A scream breaks forth on soprano sax – the crucial slice, the deadly slash. The bass bows mournful, the tubas see the bull's staggering fall. With pocket trumpet the matador receives the crowd's thunderous applause.

The bottom stirs with oboes and bassoons. The bull in its agony struggles to rise. Steeped in the crowd's adoration, the matador ignores the shrill warning flutes. With gargantuan effort the bull rises and gores the matador from behind. They both crumple in a heap. The crowd goes mad, wild . . .

'Damn! I need a whole orchestra for this one,' said J.A.

Preoccupied with this, he wandered into an inviting narrow alley.

A neon sign blinked 'Dolores' VIP Lounge'.

A slender man blocked J.A.'s way to the door.

'My man,' the stranger said. 'It's been a long time. How you doin'?'

He had a long lean face, slanted eyes and the overall appearance of a wolf dressed in a pink suede suit, black felt hat and pointy shoes.

J.A. could not place the man. But the type was familiar. A pimp.

'Hey – what it is!' he greeted. 'What you doin' out here tonight? You tryin' to catch?'

'That's right,' the stranger said. 'Tonight's the night.'

'Beautiful, man. You been inside?'

'Oh, yeah. They're all in there. Looks sparse, but don't let it fool you, my man.'

They slapped hands and J.A. entered Dolores' VIP Lounge alone.

A bar ran almost the length of a long, dark, narrow room. There were a few tables in the aisle and some dimly perceived booths in the back. A standard bar scene.

But this place had a curious flavour he could not define. Perhaps it was the subdued violet lighting, the patchwork linoleum floor or the left-over Christmas lights on the wall opposite the bar.

Aside from a little cheap tinsel, the place was stark. A jukebox glowed silently in the back. The stale wind of abruptly halted conversations rattled against the wall, then died. J.A. took a prominent seat at the nearly empty bar.

Only two other people were drinking at the bar, sitting at opposite ends, facing each other. One was an old man dressed in grey overcoat, grey felt hat with feather, his face sunken and colourless. The face of a crone – completely gaunt with heavily lidded piercing grey eyes and drawn cheeks, a large hooked nose and a shapeless, probably toothless mouth. Frail as a bird, he perched unsteadily at the front end of the bar, his back facing the door.

At the other end sat a woman, short and dumpy-looking. From her revealed arms hung loose and pitted flesh. A thick lacquer of make-up disguised her true origins. Her hair was piled in that popular 1950s fashion, the beehive. Whether or not this orange tangle above her painted face was a wig, J.A. could not decide. Clearly, her eyelashes were false, her breasts saggy, and her waistline indeterminate in the washed-out shiny print dress.

Yet she was not entirely unattractive. J.A. nodded to her as he waited anxiously for a bartender. There must be someone whose function was to cater to this motley clientele. The woman nodded, merely acknowledging J.A.'s presence, and made a clucking sound with her tongue and teeth. The elderly gaunt gentleman peered into the glass before him.

A door banged, loud footsteps came nearer, and a heavy-set

red-faced man in a discoloured T-shirt approached the bar. He brushed by the woman, speaking softly to her, then ducked under the bar to assume his station.

J.A. despised him on sight. Those beefy arms, pawlike hands, coarse black hair curling on his chest and forearms repulsed him. The man's features were crude. Two welts that had a permanence about them lined his square jaw. The hair on his head was also coarse and cropped short. His stomach hung over his pants and his shoulders were broad and powerful.

'No one to mess with,' thought J.A. 'One drink, maybe two, but no way will I tarry here long.'

The bartender addressed him. 'Hope you didn't wait too long. Had to check the basement.'

'That's OK,' J.A. replied, 'we were all just getting acquainted.'

'What'll it be?'

'Give me a tall vermouth. On the rocks.'

'Dry or sweet?' inquired the bartender.

J.A. scrutinized him. This bartender had the air of a butcher. All he lacked was the bloodied apron.

'Dry, always dry,' said J.A. 'I never touch the sweet.'

'Let's see,' said the bartender, searching the shelves high and low. 'Sorry, we're out. Want anything else?'

'Give me some dinner wine then. Got any dinner to go along with it?'

'Dinner wine?' The bartender's voice, guttural, became sceptical.

'Yeah, burgundy, red wine. Vino fino. Nothing sweet.'

'You want dinner? There's a place about three blocks away.'

'No. Forget dinner. Just the wine.'

The bartender reached into the cooler and hoisted a jug with a red and white label, checkered like a tablecloth in an Italian restaurant.

'Will this do?' he asked.

'That'll *do*,' said J.A.

The bartender filled a glass and set it before J.A. He picked it up and inhaled it before the man had a chance to put the jug away. He motioned for another wine, which was poured. This time the bartender left the jug out near the cash register.

Burgundy did not quite achieve the desired effect, the one he got from cheap vermouth. It only warmed him a bit. The second glass drained, he ordered another. The third glass, he took with him to the jukebox and pushed some buttons at random. A rhythm-and-blues number came on.

'Care to dance?' he asked the woman. He'd noticed her watching him closely.

The woman slid off the stool. 'My name is Maude.'

'Maude,' he said, tipping his hat and offering his hand. 'J.A. Blevins.'

He put his wine down on the bar next to her glass. His eyes swept over her an instant before he began leading her around the floor. Maude was short, as short as a child. Spike heels gave her extra inches and the towering hairdo added another six or seven.

He put his arm around her waist, having to stoop to do this, and let the other hand rest on her shoulder. Their steps were erratic but honed to the beat. Maude stepped righteously, with a cute waddle that J.A. could not resist. He pinched her wide flattened behind.

She let out a shriek, gave him a quick stinging slap on the cheek and climbed on to her barstool, pushing his glass as far from her as the length of her arm permitted.

'Forgive me,' said J.A. 'I meant no harm.'

'Go to hell,' said Maude.

'Beehive woman, really, I meant no harm.'

'The name is Maude.'

At this point the bartender intervened. 'You,' he said to J.A., 'settle down.' Thick forearms folded over his chest, he continued, 'You come to drink here, or you come to stir things up?' Now he unfolded his arms and leaned threateningly on the bar. 'This here's a peaceful place. No trouble with the cops, no trouble with the customers. You want to drink here, you settle down.' Unfolding his arms, he slowly patrolled his domain behind the bar.

'Nobody tells me what to do.' J.A. was about to expound on this statement when Maude addressed the bartender.

'Frank, listen to that fool. He thinks nobody can tell him what to do. He's a real fool, don't you think, Frank?' She turned to J.A. 'Who do you think you are, anyhow, somebody special? Just 'cause you're here in this bar drinking like the rest of us, that make you special? Fact is, there's always somebody telling you what to do 'less you own the whole world. And you don't look like you own nothing.' Her voice was dry and throaty. 'Direct or indirect, somebody's always telling you something. You got to listen now and then or your life ain't worth a damn dime.'

He looked at her. 'Forgive me madam, I can hardly believe such words have come from your lovely mouth. Again, forgive me, I disagree.'

Settling back on his barstool J.A. began enjoying himself.

At last, the gaunt old man spoke.

'Frank, I'll take care of the next one.' A crisp dollar bill in his bony hand, he pointed to J.A., who made no gesture or response.

The bartender was inert, but the old man waved his money so insistently that Frank hoisted up the jug one more time, poured a fresh glass and set it down with offhand clumsiness. Several wine drops spilled into a pool around the glass. Reluctantly but efficiently he blotted it with a rag right under J.A.'s nose.

'This one's on the Senator,' said the bartender.

J.A. looked up. 'Who?'

'The Senator,' Frank repeated, pointing to the old man.

Taking his newly poured wine, J.A. resettled on a barstool closer to the Senator, raising his glass. 'To you, Senator. Your health! . . . By the way, Senator of what?'

'The people, naturally, their representative, Illinois State,' said the Senator in a cracked voice, '1912 to 1922. You weren't born yet, sonny.'

'Thanks for the drink.' Damn, he thought, looking closely at the Senator, this is one hoary motherfucker. The Senator's skin adhered to his face like the puckered wallpaper in J.A.'s hotel room. Very casually, he asked, 'Senator of why?'

The Senator sombrely answered, 'To withstand enormous pressure at the city's gates; to not withstand the woman's loving arms; to stand by my sons who died on the shores of France.'

'You been to France, Senator?'

'Can't say I have, young man.' No one had called J.A. 'young man' in years. 'Speak up, young fellow. Or sit closer.'

'Can you hear me now?' J.A. said loudly.

'Nope. Wait a minute.'

The Senator leaned on his cane and dug into a shopping-bag on the floor. He rummaged around until he pulled forth an ear trumpet which he placed on the bar. Using his cane to aid him, he recovered his position on the barstool. J.A.'s fingers brushed over this ancient heavy plastic instrument coloured an off-shade of pea-green.

The Senator lifted it to his ear and said, 'Now.'

'Now is right, Senator. The time is always now. What better time than this moment for capturing the essence, squeezing the juices from the notes dictating the rhythm of all life? I mean, the music! Senator, I too, play the trumpet by ear.'

The old man looked intrigued. 'You don't say?'

'Senator of how?' J.A. asked.

'You know the how. I know the how-less.'

'Whatever that means,' J.A. told him.

'We will never know,' responded the Senator.

'Allow me to buy you a drink, Senator!' Utterly pleased by the Senator's reply, J.A. clapped him on the back, nearly knocking him off the barstool, for the Senator was fragile and weighed no more than ninety pounds. In childlike enthusiasm, J.A.'s fist crashed down on the bar.

'*Innkeeper! More wine!*' he demanded.

Frank regarded him icily. 'I found your wine,' he said.

'What?' said J.A. and the Senator simultaneously.

'Look, buddy.' Frank held up that white-and-silver-labelled tall green bottle. 'Isn't this your specialty? I just happened to find one in the back. Want it?'

'What's the Senator drinking?'

'The usual,' said Frank.

'The usual,' echoed the Senator.

'Now, what'll it be, buddy? Red dinner wine or this here?'

J.A. pointed decisively at the dry vermouth. 'A tall glass, on the rocks.'

'This stuff ain't soda pop,' said Frank.

'And,' said J.A., 'send a drink for the lady, with my compliments. What does the lady drink, sir?'

'Old-fashioneds.' Annoyed with himself for having answered, Frank leaned over and grabbed J.A.'s shirt-front with a hairy fist. 'Hey buddy, I ain't no go-between. Remember that.' He released J.A. and stepped back, arms folded across his belly.

J.A. was about to make a venomous reply, but the Senator pulled his sleeve.

'Aw, Frank doesn't mean anything, sonny. He calls everyone "buddy". Didn't hurt you, did he? Frank does get a bit familiar. Long as I can remember he's been like that . . . I remember quite a ways back, sonny, for ever . . .'

'I'll bet,' J.A. answered.

'No thanks, don't gamble any more.' The Senator chuckled.

'You still get horny, Senator?'

A pinkish tinge welled up in his grey hollowed features. 'Yep.' He blushed.

'Damn,' said J.A.

Frank brought the drinks, menace in his walk. 'That'll be four dollars,' he snarled.

J.A. pulled out his last twenty and handed it to Frank. 'Respectfully,' he said. 'Sir,' he said. 'Innkeeper.'

Frank moved to the cash register, keeping eye contact with J.A. even while he counted out the change. 'Like I said, this place is peaceful, just like a green valley.'

'Like a rest home for faggots, you mean.'

'Look, nigger . . .'

'I knew you'd call me that sooner or later. How predictable you are, how stupid.'

'If you don't like it here, leave.'

'I refuse to leave.'

'Suit yourself.' Frank turned his back and walked to Maude's end of the bar.

The Senator was fidgeting with a contraption he'd inserted in his ear. He pressed a button on the small box in his hand. 'The waters shall rise,' he intoned. 'The city shall be in danger for it is clay and rests on crumbling feet.' There was prophetic fervour in the Senator's eyes. He finished his drink. 'Catastrophic, catastrophic . . .' The Senator fell into a troubled silence.

'*Innkeeper*, more wine!' J.A. demanded.

Frank picked up the tall green bottle. 'Thirsty tonight, aren't you?'

'Always thirsty for this stuff. Leave that bottle right here.' J.A. indicated the precise spot on the bar. 'It's almost empty. Got another bottle?'

'Sure. But you'll have to pay for it now.'

'I'll pay.'

'You bet you will.'

'I already paid more than this stuff's worth.'

'What would you know about good stuff?'

'*Innkeeper*, do you know who I am? Do you realize who you're talking to?'

Frank raised a bushy eyebrow, revealing a swarthy scar across his eyelid that J.A. hadn't noticed before. 'Now you're a big celebrity. Is that it?'

'Can *you* play?'

'Sure, buddy, I can play.' Frank scowled, then laughed.

J.A. laughed. The Senator emerged from shrouded silence, laughed.

Maude, sitting all by herself, laughed so hard she nearly lost a false eyelash in her old-fashioned. She slid off the barstool doubled over with laughter, holding herself. 'It hurts, ha ha ha ha ha, it hurts.' She was choking.

Like lightning, Frank was around the bar to attend to Maude, walking her up and down in his sheltering arms. Finally she ceased the laughter that had become painful. Frank helped her on to a chair by a table in the aisle and brought her fresh water which she gratefully drank. He sat down with her, patted her back comfortingly. 'Maude,' he said, 'I was worried there for a minute.'

'Me too,' she said.

He gave her an encouraging smile. 'Better now?'

She nodded and together they walked back to the bar. This time she took a stool closer to J.A. and the Senator.

'*Innkeeper*!' J.A. bellowed. 'Drinks for the house. Buy yourself one too. On me.'

'Oh, no,' said the Senator, 'it's my turn, I insist. Maude, my dear, are you fully recovered?'

'Yes . . . yes . . . I'm fine. But it reminded me of the house next door to where I grew up . . .' She looked far away as though she saw it. '. . . there was an iron gate. Behind the gate was a yard with the fiercest dogs you could imagine, three of them. Now, a middle-aged couple lived there. Their children used to play with those beasts, but the kids grew up and went away.

'. . . Only other person who came in that gate was a messenger. He turned those horrible beasts into cute little puppies with just a glance. Then one day all three vicious animals lay stinking dead in the yard. Looked like poison to me, looked fishy.'

Maude looked J.A. in the eye and continued.

'. . . After that, an old woman dressed in rags, with dusty and bleeding feet, came into the yard, put her shopping-bags down on the porch and knocked on the door.'

J.A. interrupted. 'Beehive woman, does your tongue do nothing but flap?'

'Let her finish,' insisted Frank.

Maude turned her head and spat three times.

J.A. needed a break from these depressing people. 'Leave the bottle, Innkeeper. I'll be back.'

Outside the VIP Lounge, a cool breeze refreshed J.A.

The moon had risen, travelled the sky and hung fat and full in the east. It shone on a couple across the street who stood entwined in sensuous embrace. They drew apart unwillingly. The mini-skirted whore walked away into the night; her pimp crossed the street. It was the same man he'd met before going in to drink. Overhead, the neon sign blinked, changing the pimp's aura from dark-green to red.

'My man. You're still here.'

'Yeah, I'm here.'

'You look a little down, my man. Smoke this.' The pimp handed him a joint. J.A. lit it in silence, inhaled, passed it back.

'Yeah . . .' J.A. appreciated the buzz. 'Where'd you find the fox?'

'Her? She's my cousin. Been playing anywhere? I used to go hear you in that club off Washington Park. At the Sutherland Hotel, too. You my main man.'

'You remember all that? That was centuries ago.'

'Got to keep up with my man. You been gone. Where to?'

'Just around the corner.'

A seed popped unexpectedly and J.A. dropped the roach. The pimp immediately stooped to pick it up. 'It's out,' he said.

'I'm cool,' said J.A. 'What's your name, blood?'

Still on his knees, the man looked up. 'Abadon Beale's the name,' he mumbled under his breath.

J.A. didn't quite hear him, but took the outstretched hand Beale offered him when he stood up.

'Hey – let me buy you a drink.'

'My main man,' exclaimed Beale and opened the door for J.A. They stepped inside.

Frank was hunched attentively in front of Maude. The Senator incanted phrases to himself, dignity in his bearing, eyes on his drink. J.A. and Abadon Beale sauntered to the back booth and sat down. J.A. lit a cigarette, offered the pack to Beale.

'What are you drinking?'

'Whatever you are is fine with me, J.A.'

Energized by the reefer, J.A. walked briskly to the bar for his bottle and glass. The Senator sat lost in thought. Frank and Maude, in intimate dialogue, ignored J.A. until he was halfway down the bar.

'You . . . know that guy?'

'Yeah, Innkeeper. What of it?'

Frank handed an empty glass to J.A. 'Here – for your . . . er . . . uh, friend.'

J.A. brought his bottle and two glasses to the booth, poured their wines. Beale looked at his watch.

'Innkeeper, we need ice!' J.A. shouted.

Beale was still studying his watch.

'Got someplace to go?'

'Matter of fact, I do have an appointment. But not quite yet. Listen, Blevins, there's not much time. Maybe you remember, maybe you don't. But *I* remember.'

'Remember what?' J.A. looked puzzled.

Frank brought the ice and hovered over them. He stared at Beale. 'You haven't been around lately.'

'Right.'

'How's business?'

'Booming.'

'Find what you were looking for?'

'I sure did . . .' Beale slid his gaze to J.A. and spoke no more to Frank, who wiped his hands on a towel as he walked away.

'What'd you call him? Innkeeper? Hah hahhah . . . pretty good, my man.'

'What do you mean about "remembering"?'

'No big thing, my man. In fact, for a long time I forgot it. But tonight, every bit came back.'

'*What* came back?'

'It was so long ago, I wasn't sure you recognized me. I figured you forgot.'

'Forgot *what*?'

'You owe me, my man.'

'Owe you? . . . I never saw you before in my life.'

'Let me freshen your memory.'

J.A. finished his wine and poured another.

'That night in Munich, Blevins . . . you remember . . .'

'Munich?' J.A. leaned forward. 'What the hell *you* doing in Munich?'

'Hearing you play, my man. Now do you remember that night? Or don't you?'

'You're crazy. I never even been in Munich.'

'Yeah, you were there . . . you and your quartet. A candle got knocked over and . . . you remember that . . .'

'You're hallucinating.'

'No way, my man. You can't deny – '

'I told you. I never been to Munich. I never seen you before.'

'You seen me. We made an agreement. Now it's time for me to collect.'

'Agreement? What agreement? I never seen you before. I never played Munich. What the hell you talking about?'

'Don't deny me, my man. You can't. You're in no position to do that.' Beale pushed up his jacket sleeve. 'See that?' A long ugly scar seamed his forearm.

J.A. recoiled. He started getting up but Beale grabbed his elbow.

'Get your damn hands off me!'

'Wait a minute now. You ain't going nowhere, Blevins. You owe me. Sit down, my man.'

They both sank back into the booth facing each other.

A shadow fell on the dim back booth where the two men sat glaring. J.A. looked up. Frank stood over them.

'I told you guys before, I don't want trouble. Get out, both of you.'

Abadon Beale stood up smoothly, looked at his watch, removed it from his wrist and threw it on the table.

'All right. Got to be on my way anyhow.'

Frank took a few steps back.

Beale looked down at J.A. 'Always a pleasure, my man. See you later. We can take care of business then, even the score. Don't be late.' And to Frank he said: 'Hope we haven't inconvenienced you. Give my best to Dolores.'

Frank made sure Beale left, then stared at J.A. who was examining the watch which he had just acquired. Shrugging his shoulders, he put it on, ignoring the bartender's angry gaze.

'The minute you walked in here I smelled trouble.'

'So what?' said J.A. 'Look, I need more wine, Innkeeper. How long you going to make me wait?'

'Wine doesn't seem to agree with you.' Frank shifted his weight.

'Wine is the very meat I crave,' replied J.A. 'The substantive infusion that lubricates pure unduplicated music.'

'You're full of crap,' said Frank, shifting his weight to the other foot. His arms were crossed and a towel draped over his shoulder.

'Innkeeper, if you don't understand, I do. I need more wine.'

'What if I refuse to serve you?'

'To serve me is your function. It's that simple.'

'Sorry. 86.' Frank started to walk away.

J.A. called after him, 'Innkeeper!'

Frank turned. 'You can sit back here if you don't cause no more trouble. But I'm shutting you off, understand? Anyone who drinks like you ought to be dead by now.'

'But I am so alive, you can hardly stand it.' J.A. was on his feet, bristling.

The Senator's voice drifted through the room. 'Snakes are alive as well, writhing in the grass, prepared with venom.'

The words were uttered in a cracked implacable voice. Perched on his barstool he sat, shrunken and frail.

There was a brief silence, then Frank walked his hard massive bulk up to J.A. 'I've seen drinkers, and I've seen *drinkers*. You better tune in on sanity – fast.'

'Innkeeper, you got a hard head. I'm sick of your statutes, your ordinances, your platitudes. *More wine*, you dig? *Wine!* Right now! *Wine! Wine!*'

'Yea, moreover, wine is a treacherous dealer,' the Senator quoted.

'No more wine,' said Frank. 'Get your ass gone before something happens you won't like.'

'Innkeeper, you can't deny me. I am a fact of your existence.'

'Out, buddy. This is my last warning.'

'Shut up, Innkeeper. Pour some wine.'

'I'll cut your tongue out and shove it down your throat first.'

'Don't you mean my balls?'

'I'll show you what I mean.'

Frank collared him. J.A.'s feet dangled in mid-air. He spat in Frank's face. Dropping him, Frank swung at his jaw. J.A. ducked just in time.

'My teeth!' he screamed, anxiously checking his chops. 'Do you know who I am?'

'I know *exactly* who you are.' Frank punched him in the solar plexus, momentarily knocking the wind out of him. J.A. fell to the floor.

Maude made her cluck-cluck sound with tongue and teeth. 'Aw, Frank,' she coaxed. 'Enough's enough.'

'Then help me get him downstairs.'

Maude minced away from her barstool and went to J.A. She and Frank grabbed him by the armpits.

'Unhand me!' hissed J.A., revived. 'I'm no piece of meat!'

'Want more wine? Then come with us.' Frank opened the basement door.

Rickety stairs led into a black hole. Giddiness overtook J.A. for a moment. The smell rising from the hole was unmistakable.

Maude stayed on the threshold as Frank pushed J.A. downstairs. The atmosphere grew damper. Fumes condensed on to their clothing. A draught blew in from somewhere. J.A. assessed the situation.

'*Wwwhhhaaattttt??????*' He turned to Maude in the upper door-way, her beehive hairdo glowing neon.

Frank shoved him down the remaining steps. The smell of wine oozed from the very walls. Frank shone a flashlight around the cellar. The streaking light revealed a stone foundation. The walls were covered with slime. The floor was slippery. J.A. struggled for balance, the flashlight in his eyes.

'You'll enjoy it down here, buddy. Just you and an infinite supply. Of wine.'

'Fantastic place, Innkeeper. Let's get back upstairs.'

'You wanted wine.'

'Yeah.'

'You're never satisfied.'

'Right.'

'Do you know who *I* am?' Frank asked. 'Heavyweight champ of the Army, 1945.' With this he belted J.A. in the stomach. Blevins folded like an accordion.

Maude called from above, 'Frank, that's enough. Come up now.'

'Shut up, woman,' he yelled, but obeyed after a glance at J.A., who was gasping in horror. How had he let this befall him?

As Frank climbed the stairs he beamed the light up at Maude. Her nakedness was revealed under the sleazy dress, her wrinkles, her flab, her textures. She stood transparent and spindly on spike heels.

'Move, woman! Quick! Call them!'

The door slammed. J.A. heard the key turn in the lock.

The stink of wine and rot sickened him.

'*Damn,' he said. ' Insanity's cellar is putrid and vile. Here, now, alone, I cannot summon the creativity who is myself to unlock this door. These ragged dogs have chained it with their teeth.'*

Depairing and disgusted, he hoped to escape before the police

came. To comfort himself, he groped to the cask, felt for the spigot, found it, and placing his mouth to it, let the wine trickle down his throat. His lips sucked the faucet and he drank many times. The wine seemed good. His thirst became ferocious, unquenchable. He drank again, and was still not slaked. He drank until the wine had infused new substance and will in him.

Only the faintest light came through a crack under the door, just enough to give the oozing droplets of wine on the dark stones a slight sheen. That this crack was the provider, the source of all his light at the moment pleased him; caused him to ponder all other cracks from which he'd gleaned nourishment, inspiration and relief.

Leaning on the cask, he listened to the wine settle in the barrel. It sounded like a slow creek on a summer's day, transported him to those leafy, lazy days in his long-ago boyhood. The stream picked up momentum, gathered force and he heard it in his ears as Niagara's torrent. He heard the wine thunder down on him, and saw himself a rock, unmoved by the onslaught, unharmed by these wild rapids of wine.

Yet he knew that some day it would erode him, and he would evaporate into the sun. But tonight, his flesh was as hard as granite. The surge and tide of wine against it made him feel incredibly strong.

A voice whispered softly, 'Darling.' The voice was heavy, seductively feminine.

'Darling.' His dick hardened and he held it in his hand. The voice spoke again. 'My darling, I'm here, take me. Do it to me. Don't make me wait all night.'

J.A. was both astounded and aroused. He wondered where the whore was, thought the voice came from inside the cask. His erection was growing painful.

'Take me, I want it, you want it . . . Come get it baby,' the voice teased.

A whore at this moment would be better than nothing. Yes, a whore would be perfect.

'Where are you?' he cried.

No answer forthcoming. Was this another of the innkeeper's weird tricks? Again the voice startled him.

'Here I am!'

J.A. moved from the cask, walked to the wall. In the thick darkness he saw nothing, but felt, detected, another presence. Something fluttered against the stones.

'You need me,' the voice sang out from the opposite wall.

'Yes, I need you,' said J.A.

The light crack in the door widened. He saw the door was

unlocked and open.

'Don't go, taste me first,' she begged.

To mount the stairs instead of this amorous, enticing female might be a great mistake. Yet he chose to move towards the light even if it meant he would be thrust into another, a further, darkness. He climbed the stairs, his dick hard as iron, wanting to stay and yet wanting to escape.

Her voice stopped him. 'Don't go darling. Stay with me! I'll give you everything!'

'Where are you? Show yourself,' he pleaded.

No answer.

'Where are you? Who are you?'

From the direction of the cask he heard the whisper.

'I'm in the wine,' she said, 'I am the wine.'

Upstairs, he saw them situated as before.

The Senator at one end of the bar, Maude at the other, facing the Senator. Frank was nowhere in sight. J.A. advanced on Maude.

'Beehive woman.' He put his arm around her. 'Now that we have tasted delights from the same spring, so to speak, let us get to know each other better.'

'Why?'

'Why is why is the answer to why,' said J.A. 'I'm attracted to you. You know that. Let us negotiate. I am not a wealthy man but I have other riches to offer you. I want some nooky, baby. How 'bout it?'

Maude sighed a weary sigh.

'I want it baby, I need it. Listen, I can pay. You want it too. You need it, I can tell. So let's get out of here . . . and . . .'

'It costs more than you can afford.'

'How do you know?'

'Up front.'

'How much?'

Maude laughed. He took advantage of her good humour to ease his hand under her buttocks resting on the barstool. She jumped up, pursed her dark red lips at him, a frown in her eyes.

'No samples,' she warned.

'How much?' he repeated.

'Five hundred.'

'What?'

'Five hundred up front or forget it. That's my price for you.'

'OK baby, for all that honey in your pot. Hah, beehive woman, hah hah . . .'

'My name is Maude,' she said.

'OK Maude, let's go to my hotel.'

'You're crazy.'

'Yes, about you. Let's go. We agreed on five hundred, right?'

J.A. sensed a heavy presence behind him. It was Frank.

'The Senator would like to have a word with you,' he said.

'Tell him I'm busy.'

'He says it's urgent.'

J.A. removed his arm from Maude's shoulder.

'We got a date,' he said and crossed the room to respond to the expectant Senator. His piercing eyes were thoroughly bloodshot.

'Sit down, son. A singular evil is afoot. I tried to warn you though you harkened not.' The words seemed to come from a great distance through the Senator's shapeless lips.

'Now they will slay you utterly,' he quoted. 'There is nought but abomination in this cauldron . . . stony hearts, ruin heaped upon desolate altars . . .'

'Excuse me, Senator,' said J.A. 'The lady and I are leaving.'

He motioned to Maude to get her coat. She remained seated. He began walking towards her. All eyes followed him.

Frank held a gun and the muzzle of the gun was aimed at J.A. He halted.

'INNKEEPER, YOU MOTHERFUCKER, MORE WINE!'

Frank pointed the gun at J.A. with one hand while the other hand reached for a tall lean bottle with silver-and-white label.

J.A. grabbed it, ripped open the metal screwcap, and downed half the bottle in a single swallow.

'C'mon baby,' he called to Maude, 'let's go.'

'What did you call her?' asked Frank.

'None of your business, Innkeeper.'

'You called her "whore"! I'll kill you for that, but you deserve worse.'

J.A. picked up the bottle, drank again. Then he broke it on the bar, held the jagged neck before him.

'That's right, I called her whore. And you're a filthy son of a – '

Frank fired the gun. The broken bottle flew out of J.A.'s hand.

'It's real peaceful in here,' Frank spat at J.A. 'You agree?'

'Yeah, real peaceful. A rest home for whores and faggots.' J.A. started backing towards the exit.

Frank aimed the gun and fired again. At that instant someone entered from the street. The door flew open, knocking J.A. aside. The bullet whizzed past him. In the doorway, Abadon Beale fell without a sound.

J.A. leaped over the body on the floor and fled down the street.

Stumbling up the hotel stairs to his room, J.A. paused to inspect the wristwatch the pimp had given him. Its red dial glowed 9.33 though the sun was just rising. 'It's never too late,' he thought, 'I got time. Time is what I'm all about.'

Chuckling, he opened his door. The same musty smell assaulted his nostrils. An empty vermouth bottle lay on the floor. Two clean sheets were tossed on the rumpled bed, a bimonthly courtesy of the management. Otherwise, the room was as he'd left it.

He sat on the bed pondering his narrow escape. A new thought churned in his mind. It seemed destiny was working in his favour – he would take the expensive watch to the pawnshop and redeem his trumpet.

Energy gusted through him. He set about in a frenzy, making the bed, wrestling the stubborn window up two inches. A hot, sooty breeze filtered in. It made him nauseous.

'I can't practise here . . . I'm gonna move! Get my horn out of the shop and go on the wagon. Get me a real fine woman. Make my comeback . . . maybe Japan . . . yeah, Japan . . . I still got connections . . .'

He felt grimy and threw his soiled shirt to the floor. 'All right, people. Watch out! J.A. Blevins is back!' He could already see his new record album, hear the pure, original, evolved music on the disc. 'Get me a real fine mama and leave this rat-hole. This marginal thing ain't happening.'

He went down the hall to the bathroom, locked the door, filled the tub. Unhesitating, he plunged into an icy bath that took his breath away. His blood ran faster, cleared his brain. In the running water he thought he heard his mother's high-pitched voice calling him. 'Supper, James Anthony, James Anthony . . .' He shut the tap. Her voice ceased. She'd been dead twenty years, but he felt her loving presence. Another good omen.

Invigorated by the bath, he wanted a drink. An awful thirst welled up in his throat. He coughed repeatedly, spat in toilet paper. There was blood on the tissue.

Cold sweat broke out on his face.

Back in the room he lay down on the newly made bed. Tunes drifted into his mind. He hummed a theme, heard it dip through the registers, end in a trill. He jumped up, found blank paper, a pen, drew in staff lines.

The notes flowed into place above, between, below the lines. Three more bars and the opening would be finished. Satisfied, he relaxed, waited for the rest to come to him.

Then he saw a blur racing against the floorboard, the wall.

The mouse.

'You back already?' he called out. 'So you're back, huh?' J.A. addressed the mouse in conversational tones. 'I guess you got to be somewhere. Just don't start acting the fool, hear?'

The mouse made no reply.

'OK. Maybe you understand.'

The mouse seemed to nod in agreement. Its bright eyes assessed him.

Irritated, J.A. continued with his composition. He needed a drink. But he continued writing until an urge to pray overwhelmed him. He knew he had a chance to make it. One last chance.

'You be my witness, mouse.'

Down on his knees by the bed, he emptied his mind, tried to pray, tried to forget his awful thirst.

'Lord, Lord. I never prayed much, but hear me now. Fear no evil, isn't that how it goes?' He glanced towards the mouse. 'Mine enemies surround me . . . yeah . . . that innkeeper . . . then that devil Beale pops up . . .' The mouse was listening intently. 'Lord, I need strength. I gotta turn this thing around.'

He was very tired and slumped on to the bed.

'Right now it's you and me, mouse, you and me . . .'

For a moment he sat bolt upright. The mouse was gone.

Exhaustion overtook him. He slept.

Blevins woke that evening to a lovers' quarrel raging in the next room. A radio blared gospel in the room below his. Outside, sirens wailed in the streets.

The breeze had sharpened into high wind that tore around the tiny room, scattering his music. He collected the precious pages, wanting to focus on the end of his new song.

He wanted a drink. He wanted a drink badly.

His hands trembled as he took a glass of water. Fatigue bore down on him. He yawned, lay down again, dropped into a fitful sleep.

He dreamed a fat blonde primping before a mirror. Pink thighs oozed between a frilly garter belt and black fishnet stockings. The impresario, Fleischmann, stuck his head inside the dressing-room.

'Five minutes, *Fräulein*.'

She continued painting herself. The drummer huddled in a corner, preparing his fix. The crowded backstage dressing-room in the Munich *hofbrau* house reeked of stale cabbage.

'You are the devil's *own* instrument, Meister Blevins,' the *fräulein* said, winking at him. She was the magician's assistant and the J.A. Blevins Quartet was appearing on the same bill. The *hofbrau*-owner hoped to double his profits this way.

Fleischmann re-entered the dressing-room.

'Ach, they are crazy with your music! You must give a fourth set. I guarantee for you and your boys ein bonus.'

'More bread, man. Overtime.'

'Anything, ja. Only agree. Next you're on . . . ein bonus, ja . . .'

The magic act performed. Then a delay – trouble with the sound system. Fleischmann went out front to appease the restless crowd.

Meanwhile, a black American dressed in a pink suede suit and dark felt hat entered the dressing-room. He gave J.A. a knowing look.

'Abadon Beale's the name, brother. Hustling's the game.' He extended a leathery palm to be slapped. 'Hey – got my eye on you – I be looking out for what you do.'

J.A. did not appreciate the man's impertinent tone. Strained, tired, he'd been drinking since breakfast. Dismissing the man with a half-hearted 'right-on' he ran through his music one last time.

Beale went out into the spacious *hofbrau* house, took a chair near the stage. Immediately he provoked a fight with someone in an adjoining booth. When the band appeared onstage, Beale's loud arguing was drowned out. The audience whistled, stamped their feet and applauded for several minutes.

Then a hush. Blevins lifted the trumpet to his lips for the first note. The music began.

An eager listener tapped the querulous pimp on the shoulder. Beale pushed the intruder. A candle fell. In the noisy argument, no one noticed a smouldering napkin. One instant later, the stage drapes were bordered in flames.

Blevins continued blowing his trumpet. Steadily, the flames crept up the curtains, encouraged by old-fashioned blade fans hung from the ceiling.

Fleischmann climbed on a table, megaphone in hand, shouting directions. No one listened. Swordlike flames sent the curtain flying in a shower of sparks on to the audience, on to the stage.

Suddenly, a massive wail filled the hall. The crowd stampeded toward the exits. J.A.'s trumpet sounded above the fracas with such clarity and heartbreak that several people paused in mid-flight to listen.

J.A. stopped playing, but the drummer beat out fierce notes, creating a tempo of hysteria. The bassist wrestled his instrument offstage. J.A. was about to follow when the pimp pulled his sleeve.

'Abadon Beale's the name, brother. Are you worth your fame? Like I said, baby, you good as dead. Dig?'

'Got no time for this – ' J.A. growled. Beale grabbed his arm.

'Blevins – it's you and me. Nothing's free. Don't mess around. It's your life or your sound.'

J.A. shook loose from Beale's grasp. A prop stored overhead crashed down, blocking the exit. Fire danced along the footlights. Flats and backdrops against the stage exploded, popped, bubbled, sent hellish gases raining down on Beale's arm. His shirt-sleeve ignited. He ripped it off, and persisted with his demonic rhymes.

'Blevins! Don't screw around – the price of your life is your SOUND!'

The drumkit exploded. The drummer sat, a zombie, mesmerized by his burning drumsticks. A spotlight tumbled down, striking the drummer's head. He fell backwards.

Abadon Beale pointed to the fallen musician. He shook J.A. . . .

Groaning in his sleep, J.A. turned over. Why did he keep dreaming this horror again and again? It was as terrifying as when it happened in Munich.

The dream changed. South America. Those grim officials, accusing him of a false passport. Showing him newspaper reports of his supposed death. He cursed them, shouted. The people in line shouted too. A woman screamed shrilly.

He coughed in his sleep, woke up. The room was dark, too dark. He heard a distant roar, like surf pounding a beach. People were crying, shouting. Something was going on outside.

'Sounds like a riot or . . . ' His thoughts were muddled, he could hardly breathe. The room was sweltering. Smoke poured in through cracks in the ill-fitting door.

As J.A. struggled out of bed, an invisible fist knocked him to the floor. He crawled to the window and collapsed. Lacking the strength to raise the resistant window, he rested his chin on the sill, gulping air. A chill ran through him. Then a surge of power. He wanted to live, had everything to live for.

He crawled to the door, pulled it open. The corridor was smoke-filled, loud and crackling, like the sound of scratchy pop guns. The stairwell below was rimmed in bright orange.

He slammed the door shut against a new barrage of smoke, desperate to grope his way back to the window. Somewhere in the darkness, he found a beam of light shining in from the street. Like a fixed star it guided him. All he had to do was make it through that dark tunnel to the window. That was his star, coming up again on the horizon. His career was going to be reborn.

He made it to the window, smashed the glass with a shoe. Heavy wind drove puffs of smoke into his face. His eyes smarted, teared. Mucus poured from his nose. He raised his head, struggling not to choke in his own vomit.

Unexpectedly the wind changed direction. He saw a crowd before his stinging eyes. People shouted. He tried to shout back but the cry died in his throat. The sea of faces below him bobbed in the glare of fire. He could see *them*. Why couldn't they see *him*?

Then everything sunk from view and J.A. heard a pleasant humming sound. The last notes of his new composition fell into place. Sweet desire to play for the crowd overwhelmed him. He yearned to express everything – their sadness, rage, pain and beauty.

Firefighters were pulling hoses into the burning hotel, raising ladders to the upper storeys, leading frightened residents to safety. Another ladder truck and the snorkel squad arrived on the scene. Night people who waited in nearby bars were drawn from their lairs and joined the crowd. A pickpocket went quietly to work. Overhead, fat rainclouds raced across the waning moon. By midnight the entire second storey was in flames. The inferno was directly below J.A.'s third-floor room.

Glass shattered, children screamed. The police attempted to establish a fire line, and push back the fast-growing mob. An elderly couple, terrified, clung to a fire escape awaiting rescue.

Firefighters descended ladders with people slung head-down over their backs. All eyes in the crowd were on one of them. This firefighter's boot slipped off a rung as the howling wind shook the aerial ladder. Calmly, he regained his balance and continued the descent.

The jolt opened J.A.'s eyes and he stared dully into the upside-down faces watching him. The firefighter felt his burden shift. On the ground he eased Blevins on to a waiting stretcher, clamped an oxygen mask on his face.

Before they lifted the stretcher into the ambulance, J.A.'s aching eyes opened for the last time. In the maze of boots and equipment on the ground, he saw a small brown mouse escaping to freedom.

A man in black felt hat and pink suede suit elbowed his way through the mob.

J.A. distinctly heard Abadon say, 'Even-steven.'

The Artist, Responding to the Work of an Older Contemporary

Robert Sargent

John C. Hodges, known as 'Rabbit' to some,
Is sitting alone in a furnished room
In a Boston rooming house. It is 1926.

He is dapper, young, black. Has a thin moustache.
From the case on the floor, he must be a musician.
A phonograph is playing New Orleans jazz,

'Texas Moaner Blues', Clarence Williams's Blue Five.
It's Bechet that he's listening to, the soprano sax.
Johnnie is tapping his foot,

And from this, and his smile, you might think
He is playing the record because he enjoys the music.
And that's true as far as it goes,

But that's not the point of his listening.
That eruption of gutsiness after the smooth glissando:
How is it done, exactly?

He puts the needle back to the saxophone solo.
That rough vibrato! When the record stops,
He opens the case on the floor, takes out his horn.

From: *Aspects of a Southern Story*, The Word Works, 1983

St Louis Blues

Patrick Biggie

Patrick Biggie was a member of the Indian Police from 1936 to 1947. After leaving India, he served as British Consul at various posts, including Havana, over a period of thirty years. He is married with six children and lives in Chichester and Spain. He was awarded the OBE in 1970.

Thomas Lincoln MacAndrew and his wife Frances left Cuba for good in 1965 carrying two small suitcases – all they were allowed to take out of the country with them. It seemed precious little to show for thirty years' hard work in Havana but then that was how people in their position were treated. They flew to Florida, where they had been far-sighted enough to buy a house and to amass sufficient funds to provide for their retirement. On their arrival at Miami from Varadero, without even ten cents for a coffee, they were welcomed by their son Thomas L. MacAndrew Jr and their daughter Christine, who had travelled from California and New Jersey respectively to greet them, to supply them with ready cash and convey them to their home at Clearwater Beach.

What would have become of them had they not been fortunate enough to have had a home to go to, relatives to meet them and funds for their future is a matter for conjecture. What they were able to take out of Cuba, under the stringent laws governing the departure of *gusanos* and others who opted to leave the island, was as nothing compared with what they were compelled to leave behind.

In Havana they had had a spacious colonial-style house set in lush tropical gardens containing a swimming-pool at the edge of a large sheltered terrace. The property and the furniture in it, along with two cars and all their personal possessions, were forfeited to the government on their departure. The MacAndrews had stayed on in Cuba for some time after almost all their friends and compatriots had already left. The company Thomas MacAndrew had founded and the business he had built up over the years were taken over and nationalized by the new regime. This regime, however, swiftly discovered that it was incapable of running the company and abandoned it to decay. The offices of the MacAndrew Import/Export Company had therefore been closed and boarded up by the local Committee for the Defence of the Revolution. Even after that happened, the MacAndrews, after giving the best years of their lives to Cuba, found the prospect of leaving was almost more than they could face, but in the end they had to give way. Life became impossible if only because they were unable to subsist on Cuban rations. Fran MacAndrew's health began to suffer.

Finally they applied for permission to leave and, after a delay of nearly a year, with many regrets and ambivalent feelings, they said goodbye to the home they had built and lived in for over a quarter of a century. For Thomas MacAndrew perhaps the hardest things to leave behind were his gold clubs and his records. He was a brilliant golfer and a connoisseur of jazz.

These two completely unrelated facets of his personality were revealed to me one afternoon at the country club where I had just had a round of golf with a *gusano*, a Cuban lawyer named Pedro Aguilar. For the benefit of the uninitiated perhaps I should pause to explain here that in Cuba *gusano* (a worm) was a term of abuse applied to those who were at variance with the policy of the new regime and felt strongly enough about it to want to leave the country even at the price of forfeiting all their worldly goods and assets.

I had gone down to the club that afternoon on the off chance, hoping that I might perhaps find someone to play with. I happened to meet Pedro Aguilar, and we went round together. Always an indifferent player, I must confess that I was no match for him. He was, by any standards, very good indeed. I did not give him much of a game and back in the changing-room I complimented him on his performance. He admitted to being the current champion of Cuba but added modestly that there was not much competition now that practically every player of note had left the island. I took an immediate liking to him. My Spanish is poor but he spoke, not perfect English, but what I might describe as fluent American.

'The best player we ever had here was a guy named Tom MacAndrew. Those were his set of clubs – the ones you see right over there. They are on offer to anyone who has twelve new golf balls to spare. He had to leave them behind like everything else he owned when he left.'

'Isn't that amazing?' I interrupted him. 'We're living in his house.'

'You're joking,' said Señor Aguilar. 'Why, Tom was a great friend of mine. We used to play together most every day. Maybe one day when I leave this goddamn country we'll be playing again together in Florida. But that won't be for at least another six months; that is if I survive a spell in the *caña*, which is what we *gusanos* have to do before we get final permission to leave. I'll have to leave these behind,' he added, looking wistfully at his own set of clubs.

'I hope you'll see him soon,' I said. 'I feel I know him in a way myself, living in his house surrounded by all his furniture and possessions. One can't help feeling that people leave behind them a kind of imprint of their personality when they abandon everything in that way.'

'Sure,' he said. 'I guess that's right. I reckon people must leave something behind them when they've lived in a home all their lives. Since you're living in his house, have you come across his collection of records? Tom must have had just about the best collection of jazz in the world. Dixieland was his specialty. I'll never forget those evenings with Tom and Fran listening to his records – Louis Armstrong, Kid Ory, Jack Teagarden, Sidney Bechet – you name it, he had it – especially Sidney Bechet. Bechet was his idol. You couldn't leave Tom's house without hearing "Petite Fleur". I don't know much about music, but I liked listening to the kind of stuff he played. I wonder if all those records are still there.'

'I don't really know,' I said. 'We only arrived here a month ago and we haven't had time to sort out everything in the house but there's a room stacked with his personal belongings. I just don't know what's there but we're going to try and get round to sorting it out one of these days.'

'What are you doing here?' Pedro Aguilar asked.

'I'm with the FAO,' I told him, 'on a year's assignment as an adviser on agricultural development. After that I'll be going on to another job in the Middle East.'

'Are you going to be here for the whole of this year?'

'Well, yes, but I shall be travelling back to the States about every three months or so to report on my work.'

'Look,' said Señor Aguilar, glancing over his shoulder and dropping his voice, 'we'd better not talk here. You never know who's listening and this place is probably bugged. Could we go outside for a minute? I'd like to ask you something.'

We left the clubhouse and walked away to a safe distance. Then Pedro Aguilar stopped, looked around again to check that no one was listening, and said, 'When Tom was leaving Cuba he handed me the challenge cup with his name engraved on it. He said, "Keep this for me, Pedro. I shan't be able to take it with me when I go but I don't want those bastards to have it. If you ever get a chance, try and send it on to me. It's something I'd like to have when I get to Florida." Do you think you could take it out of the country when you travel and send it on to him? They don't check people like you when you have to travel.'

Looking ahead, I knew that my wife and I would be going up to New York in a couple of months' time. It was probably a bit irregular taking confiscated property out of the country but I agreed to do what I had been asked. It seemed to me a very harmless favour.

We walked back to the changing-room and when we were ready I said, 'Señor Aguilar, would you like to come back and have a drink at our house – I mean Tom MacAndrew's house – I don't think I should call it "our house", but you know what I mean.'

'I sure appreciate it,' said Señor Aguilar, 'but I hope you will understand if I say "no". When this situation arose I made a kind of resolution. I said to myself – I'm not going to accept any hospitality that I'm not in a position to return. It may sound crazy but I've stuck to that ever since.'

'But,' I protested, 'it's not a question of any return. It's just a matter of dropping in for a drink and I'm sure you'll be happy to see Tom MacAndrew's house again – '

'I'm sorry,' he broke in, 'I wouldn't be happy at all. Please don't get me wrong. It's sure kind of you to ask me but I have to say "no". I feel very strongly about this. Maybe you'll understand how I feel when I tell you I haven't seen my wife and kids for over six years. But I'm going to stick this out until I get out of here and then, by the grace of God, I'll start living again.'

I left him with tears in his eyes and drove back home to find my wife Lucy looking hot and tired. I asked her what she had been doing while I had been out playing golf.

'I'm just going to have a dip in the pool to cool off,' she said. 'I'll tell you what I've been doing. I thought I'd have a go at tidying up that storeroom but I just had to give up. One can't really do much in this heat. To get any kind of order out of the chaos in there would be a full day's work and I really don't feel I can tackle it on my own.'

'What's in there?' I asked her.

'What isn't in there?' was her reply. 'It's fascinating in a way. I've only scratched the surface but enough to discover a kind of museum of a family called MacAndrew. I suppose they must have lived here for years. You have no idea. There are pictures, diaries going back for years, albums of family photographs, golf cups, books and records –

hundreds and hundreds of records, all covered with mildew from this damp heat. There are some nice things in there but they'll need an awful lot of sorting out.'

'But what's the purpose of doing it?' I asked her.

'I don't quite know what the point is,' Lucy said, 'I just feel that if you live in a house you might as well know what's in it. And I thought perhaps that if we cleared up things a bit we might be able to use that room, though heaven knows where we're going to find room for all that stuff. But we might like to have a look at the books and if there's anything we can't use we might stack it up in the spare garage.'

'How far did you manage to get with it?' I asked.

'Well, I started on the books but it wasn't only the heat that put me off. I kept on hearing the sound of music coming from the back of the room. The place is so piled up with junk that I couldn't trace where the sound was coming from, but it was all so strange. As a matter of fact I was rather frightened. I don't like things that can't be explained.'

'What kind of music?'

'It was jazz. I can't say more than that. It doesn't *matter* what kind of music. The point is: where was it coming from? It's not that I didn't like it; in fact it was rather pleasant, or it might have been – music while you work – but this was·so inexplicable. I found it rather eerie.'

'I can't explain it at all,' I said, 'but anyway, let's have a swim now. I suggest we leave this until the weekend when I can help you. It's much too hot to tackle this kind of job during the day. Let's get up really early on Sunday and we'll have a go at it together and try and sort out the MacAndrews' possessions.'

We had a swim in the pool together, which did us both good, and then we sat out on the terrace with our glasses of iced Bacardi and fresh lime juice, the ideal drink for the Caribbean.

'It's funny about that jazz you claim to have heard,' I told Lucy, 'because this afternoon I was playing golf with a Cuban lawyer called Aguilar, a very good golfer. He's what they call a *gusano*. He said he was a friend of the MacAndrews before they left Cuba. Another thing he said was that Tom MacAndrew was a connoisseur of jazz and had a fabulous collection of records. His speciality was Sidney Bechet.'

'Yes, of course, that was what I heard. I couldn't put a name to it before, but now you mention it, that was what it was. Didn't we have a record of Bechet playing "Petite Fleur"? But this wasn't "Petite Fleur" – I know what it was: the "St Louis Blues".'

180

B Flat, Bebop, Scat

On Sunday we were up at dawn. The heat of the day had not really got under way though it was nearly always humid and muggy in Havana, except for a short period during the winter. We put on our swimming-suits to tackle the job, ready to plunge into the pool and cool off when the heat became unbearable. It was just as well, as the room we were going to clear up was dark and airless. We got busy shifting piles of books, picking out some that we thought we might like to read, chucking out bundles of old magazines, trying to salvage photograph albums and masses of other personal belongings that had been abandoned by the MacAndrews on their departure. When we had worked our way through these we came to the records – literally hundreds of them.

'Let's take a break now,' I suggested, 'and have a swim before breakfast.'

It was gorgeous to dive into the pool and cool off after working for a couple of hours in that stuffy room. Meanwhile our cook, a girl called Rosa, had laid the table and as soon as we were out of the pool breakfast was ready. We began with fresh grapefruit picked that very morning from the tree in the garden and then went on to coffee, toast and marmalade, in no hurry to return to the job we had set ourselves to do, and if possible complete, before lunchtime. It was already getting hotter and I was feeling relaxed when Lucy said, 'I suppose we'd better return to the fray, but let's just have a cigarette before we get down to work again.'

We lit up, poured ourselves another cup of coffee and then, as we sat there on the terrace, there came to us from the open door of that room the sad strains of the 'St Louis Blues'. I think it is a terribly difficult thing to find words to describe music but I will try to give some idea of what it sounded like.

It began, in the manner of most Dixieland numbers, with a fairly straight trumpet lead backed by a good solid tailgate man on trombone and then, when the main themes had been stated, the moment came for the first solo to take over. The entry of the clarinet at that point was sensational; it might be described as a low-down, dirty growl followed by a passage played in the lower register with that kind of 'shake' or vibrato that was the hallmark of one man only; leading and soaring upwards into the higher register, wailing, lyrical and sorrowful, to be broken by the trombone asserting itself, gruff and robust in a series of insistent repeated phrases powerfully improvised with infinite sadness. There followed a short bridge passage on piano which linked the two preceding solos with the final contrapuntal ensemble; trumpet leading once more, that driving trombone backing up behind and, as the third part of the front line, that beautiful clarinet weaving freely in and around the basic melody.

I am no expert on jazz, but no one could possibly fail to identify the touch of the one and only Sidney Bechet.

The music ended and there was silence.

'Good God,' I said, stubbing out my cigarette. Lucy was too shaken to move from where she was sitting, but I got up, walked across the terrace and from the glare of the hot sun I entered again that dark, dusty room. There was not a sound. In the half light the only movement was that of a large lizard patrolling the walls in search of prey.

Then Lucy came to the door and called to me. 'I can't face it. It's too uncanny.'

I felt a bit the same myself but I turned and said, 'Look, don't come in here, but just let me get these things out into the light of day and then we'll think again.'

It took me two hours to sort out those records. I tidied them up, cleaned them and finally stacked them back in their rightful place on the shelves of the living-room, which had obviously been designed to take them. There must have been at least thirty recordings by Bechet among them. I went through those carefully and finally found what I was looking for: a 1944 recording of the 'St Louis Blues', the version he made with Sidney de Paris on trumpet, Vic Dickenson on trombone, Art Hodes on piano, Manzie Johnson on drums and George 'Pops' Foster on bass.

A month or so later Lucy and I were on our way to spend a week in the States before returning to Havana. At that time, as far as I recall, there were only three routes out of Cuba, apart from the flights from Varadero to Miami for departing *gusanos*. First there was the Russian service to Moscow, then there was the Iberia flight to Madrid and third the Cubana service to Mexico City, from where we travelled on to New York.

At the bottom of my suitcase I have to confess that I carried two unauthorized items in my luggage. Naturally I wondered at the time whether this was a justifiable abuse of privilege on my part as a member of an international organization exempt from control by virtue of quasi-diplomatic status.

One item was Tom MacAndrew's challenge cup, which Pedro Aguilar had concealed at the bottom of his bag of clubs and handed over to me at a spot out of sight of the clubhouse while we were playing a round of golf together on the day before I left for New York.

The other was the record of the 'St Louis Blues' which, from the evidence, strange as it may seem, must, I suppose, have been Tom MacAndrew's favourite recording.

I mailed both these things to him at his address in Clearwater

Beach while we were staying in New York. There was no time for him to write and acknowledge safe receipt but I felt he got them all right. In any event I can say that we never heard the sound of the 'St Louis Blues' again during the year we spent in the MacAndrews' house in Havana. I hope it's not too whimsical to suggest that that record, like a dog that has strayed from home, had, in the long run, found its way back to its master.

Dance Harlem Style

Avotcja

I'm gonna dance away the garbage heaps up & down Eighth Avenue
I'm gonna start me a movement revolution
    & clean out all the rats with rhythm
And when I dance out in the street with all that soul plus conga beats
All the roaches gonna split
    You know, music really ain't their kick
It disturbs their solemn cosmic moods
IT'S ENOUGH TO GIVE A ROACH THE BLUES!

I'm gonna dance away the street lights,
    the police lights & the street fights
I'm gonna work a little Juju . . . dance till even Harlem sees the moon
And even all the pimps & hookers stop their hustling
    just to peek my foot-work
I'm gonna revive the old Pied Piper so the buzzard can die twice
    and then pass out from shock & fright
When he checks out all my latest leaps
    and the trash & roaches ten feet deep
On their way downtown
    where 'they' belong
        on Forty-Second Street

I'M GONNA DANCE AWAY THE GARBAGE HEAPS!

The Poets

Avotcja is a musician/singer/writer/photographer who has been performing professionally since she was fourteen. She is the author of several books and has been published in many anthologies in both English and Spanish. She lives and works in San Francisco.

David Kennedy was born in 1959 in Leicester, where he still lives. Since graduating from Warwick University he has been variously employed as a farm labourer, temporary civil servant and stock controller. He is currently preparing a collection of his poetry.

Sue May is a Londoner, and has been a member of Hackney Writers' Workshop since 1978. She regularly reads with the workshop, the Vera Twins (a women's poetry performance group) and Contradictions (a workshop-based group performing music and poetry). She has had poems and stories published in *Hackney Writers' Workshop III* and *Where There's Smoke*, as well as in numerous magazines.

David Pepperell is an Australian, born in Adelaide in 1945. After starting his own record shop in 1971, he became a regular contributor of articles to the underground press and published a book, *Raphael Alias*, in 1976. He has had his songs recorded by several artists and in 1984 won the Australian Film Industry Award as the co-composer of the best soundtrack of the year.

Anthony Revo was born in 1957 in Cornwall. A poet and a saxophonist, he lives in Bristol.

Robert Sargent was born and brought up in the South of the US, but now lives in Washington. He has published three books of poetry, the last being *Aspects of a Southern Story* (1983). His other interests include pictorial art and jazz.

Willa Woolston, artist and illustrator, was born in Philadelphia, and took up residence in London after three years at Chelsea School of Art and one at City and Guilds. Her reputation is based largely on her skill at emphasizing the 'live' aspects of her subjects, and she is a familiar sight at London jazz venues, where she draws artists in action.